THE LONDON ENGLISH

General Editor: G. C. ROSSER M.A.

THE POET'S TALE

An Anthology of Narrative Poetry

THE POET'S TALE

An Anthology of Narrative Poetry

Chosen and edited by

A. A. EVANS M.A.

HODDER AND STOUGHTON
LONDON SYDNEY AUCKLAND TORONTO

ISBN 0 340 07594 5

First published in this edition 1957
Eleventh impression (with amendments) 1976

Printed and bound in Great Britain for
Hodder and Stoughton Educational,
a division of Hodder and Stoughton Ltd, London,
by Hazell Watson & Viney Ltd, Aylesbury, Bucks

FOREWORD

There are many ways of reading literature. We can dip into a novel to pass the time away, we can give ourselves to a writer to escape from boredom or the monotony of films and television, we can read plays, short stories, and poems simply because we have developed a habit and would not be without our weekly instalment of reading. We can also read to make ourselves more mature by living through the emotional experience of other minds in this or another country. But whichever attitude we adopt, there is always one element which keeps us fascinated in literature. That element is pleasure. We read because, generally speaking, we find it pleasurable to read and the more pleasure we find in reading the more the activity becomes part of our daily lives.

What many of us have realised, of course, is that pleasure and understanding go hand in hand—the more we possess a book, the more we come to grips with its essence, the more satisfaction it gives us. The experience becomes more relevant, more urgent. However, there are some books which we suspect contain more pleasure than we are able to extract. Their spirit seems to elude us. But with some guidance, we feel, we could possess a novel or a play or a poem and retain its genius. With such assistance in mind the present series has been edited to bring before the reader an opinion which may serve as a starting-point for discussion and fuller understanding. Each volume has a commentary or introduction which endeavours to look at a piece of literature as living imaginative experience. In this respect, therefore, it may be reassuring to find that with someone else's guidance before us we begin to see with a new and deeper perception. Our sympathy has developed, the satisfaction becomes more lasting.

G. C. ROSSER

CONTENTS

Part One

BALLADS OLD AND NEW

Part Two

NARRATIVE POEMS

Part Three

EXTRACTS FROM LONGER NARRATIVE POEMS

*With a tale forsooth he cometh unto you, with
a tale which holdeth children from play, and
old men from the chimney corner.*

SIR PHILIP SIDNEY

INTRODUCTION

NARRATIVE POETRY

EVERYBODY at all ages loves a story. Long before he can read, the infant is at his happiest just before bed-time when his mother tells him a story, or reads one to him and describes the pictures in the book. At the infants' school, one of his happiest lessons is when the teacher puts all the books away and tells a story to the class. As the child learns to read, so the first thing he reads are stories, stories of imaginary animals like Peter Rabbit or of half-legendary heroes like Robin Hood—and he has started on a life-long activity—stories in papers and magazines, adventure stories, short stories, stories in newspapers and novels, grave and gay, ephemeral and 'classical'.

So has it always been, throughout the ages; for all primitive peoples, thousands of years ago just as to-day, possessed a rich store of legends of the deeds of their gods and their tribal heroes which were told around the fire or in the long dark evenings. These stories were not written down, but remembered from father to son, or they were the special responsibility of the bard or the minstrel whose job it was not only to tell of the deeds of the gods and the heroes in the traditional narratives, but also to compose new songs extolling the feats of living heroes. As the tribe or nation became more organised and more conscious of its greatness, so its poetry became more elevated and more noble, the poet more conscious of his mission as the singer of the glories of the gods and heroes. Homer's *Iliad* and *Odyssey* are outstanding examples, and they are of the world's greatest poetry. Another example of such poetry is *Beowulf*, which our ancestors brought with them when they came from the Continent to Britain after the departure of the Romans. *Beowulf* is a long epic poem, relating the deeds of one of their greatest heroes, and it is written not in simple, artless verse but in a highly sophisticated verse, with a formal pattern of metre and alliteration, and an extremely rich vocabulary and imagery.

On a lower level, but none the less true poetry, we have the incom-

parable richness of the old ballads, particularly those of Scotland and
the Border country, passionate, dramatic and highly coloured, singing
of love and battle, of adventure by sea and land, of bravery and
honour. Even after the development of 'court' poetry, the ballads
continued their vigorous life as the poetry of the ordinary people, and
still enjoyed a vigorous life in the sixteenth century, for Sir Philip
Sidney, in *An Apologie for Poetrie*, says:

> Certainly, I must confesse my own barbarousness, I never heard
> the olde song of *Percy* and *Douglas* that I found not my heart
> mooved more than with a Trumpet; and yet it is sung by some
> blinde Crouder, with no rougher voyce than rude stile.

This particular kind of ballad poetry lingered on for many years
after Sidney's time. The Irish poet W. B. Yeats wrote a fascinating
essay on *The Last Gleeman* of Ireland, who died in 1846, and Edwin
Muir, the distinguished poet and critic whose childhood was spent in
the Orkneys, tells us in his *Autobiography* of the ballads which his mother
used to sing to him, one of which began:

> Of all the ancient Scottish knights
> Of great and warlike name
> The bravest was Sir James the Rose,
> That knight of mickle fame.

As for the popular narrative poems of the streets, *The Death of
Nelson* (p. 27) shows that it was maintaining a vigorous existence in
the early nineteenth century. Events of national importance were
celebrated in verse, crude but often vivid and racy, and printed copies
were sold in the streets and shops right up until our own time. One
important piece of evidence for this is the investigation of Henry
Mayhew into the life of the street-traders. He describes, among others,
the 'Long-Song Seller' who sold songs in the London streets, and sang
them too. He quotes the words of the song-seller:

"I sometimes began with singing or trying to sing, for I'm no vocalist, the first few words of any song, and them quite loud. I'd begin:

> '*The Pope he leads a happy life*
> *He knows no care*'—

'Buffalo gals, come out tonight', 'Death of Nelson' . . ."

Students and collectors of folk poetry discovered that the tradition lived on, and still does, in the pits, the factories and the trawlers. And the tradition found new ground in the pioneering era of the United States and continued in the factories, the cotton fields, the railways and the prairie. The popular interest continues unabated, as shown by radio and television programmes and the founding of many 'folk' clubs.

In an anthology of this length and intention, it is difficult to do justice to the ballad, and impossible to do it to the great wealth of narrative in English poetry. I have therefore included some familiar narrative poems as well as others possibly not so familiar. The selection is not made on historical grounds: that is, poems are not included because of their importance as representing a particular period or 'school' of poetry (whatever that may mean), or representative in any way at all except on the broadest lines as representative of the great riches of English narrative poetry. There are, inevitably, many omissions, and, as with all anthologies, every adult reader will wish that this poem or that had been included.

Another problem of selection arises from the fact that many of the greatest English narrative poems are far too long to be included in full. Should the anthology therefore be restricted to short poems? Is there a risk of 'bittiness' in the inclusion of extracts? To exclude the long narrative poems might well mean that there would be a quite inadequate emphasis on the note of 'high seriousness' and that moral nobility which is so eminent a feature of English poetry. I have therefore included not only several fairly long and complete narratives, but also some longish extracts from five of our greatest long poems. I hope that these selections are substantial enough to be read for themselves and that they will not require much explanation as to how they fit into the whole poem.

But, above all, these poems have been chosen for the pleasure and profit of the reader, and the profit, it is hoped, will arise from the pleasure. The young reader may, of course, have to face an examination on the poems at the end of the year, but I am quite sure that an examination should not spoil the pleasure. Examinations never spoilt mine, and indeed, in a way, they helped to increase the pleasure because I had to study the poems in *depth*, and get to know them thoroughly, and I know this to be true for many of the boys and girls whom I used to teach. Many of these poems are easy to understand, others more difficult: but ease or difficulty of understanding has never been a test of quality in any of the arts. We do not expect to understand a symphony the first time we hear it played. We begin to understand it only after *listening* to it carefully a number of times. So, too, with much poetry. The more we read and re-read a great poem, the more we understand it, the more meanings we see in it, the more meaning it has for us.

There are many ways of telling stories, and many reasons why men want to tell them. *The Three Ravens* and *The Twa Corbies* are substantially the same story, but the first is gentle and pleasant in tone, the second harsh and bitter. One poem, for example, *The Pardoner's Tale*, tells a medieval story racily and rapidly, with a grim irony expressed in the situation: another, like *Morte d'Arthur*, makes a story of medieval magic convincing through its vivid imagery, both visual and aural. Another, like *Flannan Isle*, is told not so much for the story, for there is very little, but for the atmosphere of mystery, even horror: the real story is only hinted at, and its real terror is left to our imagination. Milton's telling of the story in *Paradise Lost* of the war in heaven, and the creation and fall of man, is an attempt to explain some of the fundamental mysteries of religion and 'to justify the ways of God to Men'. Wordsworth, in *The Prelude*, gives us his spiritual autobiography, to show us how he came to be what he was. Pope in *The Rape of the Lock* is brilliant, and satirical about the society of his time, its scandals and artificialities, but it is a society in which he delights.

Above all, it is important to remember that these narratives are *poems*. They are not merely stories put into verse, with a few metaphors and similes added to make them vivid, and it is quite wrong to say, as one candidate in G.C.E. once said, 'after a lot of fine writing, he comes at last to the point', as though the 'fine writing' was a self-indulgent frill. Most of these poems have very little narrative *plot*, and if one tried to extract the story from the poem, there would be only the briefest story, and indeed, in some cases, hardly any story at all. For it is the poetry which makes the story, creates its atmosphere, stresses the significant points of description, character or action, through the stanza form, the rhythm, the imagery. The mere story of Wordsworth's *Michael* is very briefly told, and put briefly and baldly, there is little more than a rather pathetic and commonplace event. But Wordsworth gives us the spiritual life and aspirations of simple, dignified peasants, revealed through their labours in a lonely countryside. The sheepfold becomes a symbol of the deep relationship of father and son and heritage. It is a revelation of dignified and noble suffering, reaching its utterly simple and profound climax in the line,

'And never lifted up a single stone', and then moving with a calmness beyond grief to its quiet end. In Arnold's *Sohrab and Rustum*, the majestic and ornate similes emphasise the fated inevitability of the conflict of father and son, and give to the poem its pathos and majesty. In *Childe Roland* the vividly described landscape is itself a living symbol and atmosphere of the evil and spiritual corruption which has trapped so many, and which Roland has to fight against, *in* himself.

The language of poetry is the most precise and efficient for the many things it has to do. It is not something vague and pretty-pretty. For precision is not exclusive to the merely matter-of-fact like 'Easter Monday is a Bank Holiday in England' or 'The square on the hypotenuse of a right-angled triangle is equal to the sum of the squares on the other two sides'. The language in those two statements is efficient: it states what it sets out to state, neither more nor less. How, then, to take a fairly simple example of poetry, can we describe as precise and efficient the following, from Coleridge's *Rime of the Ancient Mariner*:

> And ice, mast-high, came floating by,
> As green as emerald?

If Coleridge had written:

> And ice, mast-high, came floating by,
> As green as green-pea soup,

he might have been justified if he had tried to be funny through deliberate bathos. For green-pea soup is liquid, opaque, warm, a yellowish-green, and vegetable, and, above all, something homely and domestic. In all these things, it is the opposite of an ice-berg. If he had said:

> And ice, mast-high, came floating by
> And it was green as grass,

he would have made a pointless comparison, for, however beautiful grass is, it differs from ice-bergs in colour, shape, degree of trans-lucency, and, completely, in association. But when he compares the ice to emeralds we are immediately, without, perhaps, even thinking about it, struck by the appositeness. For both are green, translucent, reflecting light in their many facets, hard, glittering, and because of these many similarities, the beauty and preciousness of the emerald are *transferred* to the ice, and we see it as great emeralds in the beautiful and strange world which Coleridge is creating.

This is only a simple example of the precision of poetic language, and is taken from its imagic qualities. But we must remember that it has many other qualities of precision in addition to that of visual imagery: we sometimes tend to emphasise the visual and neglect the aural, in which meaning is expressed through sound and rhythm, and the constructive, or as it might be called, to use Matthew Arnold's word, 'architectonic', in which both visual and aural unite with the whole structure to give the full meaning. In the end, a narrative poem is not merely a story: nor is the story the only thing of importance. It is a part of the poem, and inseparable from the poem.

Part One

BALLADS OLD AND NEW

ST. STEPHEN AND KING HEROD

Saint Stephen was a clerk
  In King Herod's hall,
And servèd him of bread and cloth
  As every king befall.

Stephen out of kitchen came
  With boar's head on hand,
He saw a star was fair and bright
  Over Bethlehem stand.

He cast adown the boar's head
  And went into the hall.
'I forsake thee, Herod,
  And thy workes all.

I forsake thee, King Herod,
  And thy workes all,
There is a child in Bethlehem born
  Is better than we all.'

'What aileth thee, Stephen?
  What is thee befall?
Lacketh thee either meat or drink
  In King Herod's hall?'

'Lacketh me neither meat ne drink
  In King Herod's hall.
There is a child in Bethlehem born
  Is better than we all.'

'What aileth thee, Stephen?
  Art wode or 'ginnest to brede?
Lacketh thee either gold or fee,
  Or any rich weed?'

'Lacketh me neither gold ne fee
  Ne none rich weed.
There is a child in Bethlehem born
  Shall helpen us at our need.'

'That is all so sooth, Stephen,
  All so sooth, I-wys,
As this capon crowe shall
  That lieth here in my dish.'

The word was not so soon said,
  That word in that hall,
The capon crew *Christus natus est*
  Among the lordes all.

'Risit up, my tormentors,
  By two and all by one,
And leadit Stephen out of this town,
  And stonit him with stone.'

Tooken they Stephen
  And stoned him in the way.
And therefore is his even
  On Christe's own day.

ANON.

wode—mad.   to brede—to lose one's wits.

The story of Stephen, the first Christian martyr, is told in *The Acts of the Apostles*, Chapters 6 and 7. It is interesting to note that the legend, as told in the ballad, is substantially different from the original except in the manner of Stephen's death.

The story is told with utter simplicity and directness, for to the people who accepted it as fact it needed no embellishment. The repetitions emphasise the bewilderment of Herod and the persistence of Stephen's faith in his vision, but in all probability they are primarily oral conventions, of help both to the teller and his audience.

THE WIFE OF USHER'S WELL

There lived a wife at Usher's well
    And a wealthy wife was she.
She had three stout and stalwart sons
    And sent them o'er the sea.

They hadna been a week from her,
    A week but barely ane,
When word came to the carline wife
    That her three sons were gane.

They hadna been a week from her,
    A week but barely three,
When word came to the carline wife
    That her sons she'd never see.

'I wish the wind may never cease
    Nor fashes in the flood
Till my three sons come hame to me
    In earthly flesh and blood!'

It fell about the Martinmas
    When nights are lang and mirk,
The carline wife's three sons came hame
    And their hats were o' the birk.

carline wife—old woman.

It neither grew in syke nor ditch
   Nor yet in ony sheugh,
But at the gates o' Paradise
   That birk grew fair eneugh.

'Blow up the fire, my maidens,
   Bring water from the well,
For a' my house shall feast this night
   Since my three sons are well!'

And she has made to them a bed,
   She's made it large and wide,
And she's ta'en her mantle her about,
   Sat down at the bedside.

Up then crew the red, red cock,
   And up and crew the gray.
The eldest to the youngest said,
   ''Tis time we were away.'

The cock he hadna craw'd but once
   And clapp'd his wings at a',
When the youngest to the eldest said,
   'Brother, we must awa'.

The cock doth craw, the day doth daw,
   The channerin' worm doth chide.
Gin we be miss'd out o' our place,
   A sair pain we maun bide.'

'Lie still, lie still but a little wee while,
   Lie still but if we may.
Gin my mother should miss us when she wakes,
   She'll go mad ere it be day.'

    syke—marsh.   *sheugh*—trench.

'Fare ye weel, my mother dear,
    Fareweel to barn and byre!
And fare ye weel, the bonny lass
    That kindles my mother's fire!'

ANON.

THE TWA CORBIES

As I was walking all alane
I heard twa corbies making a mane.
The tane unto the tither did say,
'Whar sall we gang and dine the day?'

'In behint yon auld fail dyke
I wot there lies a new-slain knight,
And naebody kens that he lies there
But his hawk, his hound, and his lady fair.

His hound is to the hunting gane,
His hawk to fetch the wild-fowl hame,
His lady's ta'en anither mate,
So we may mak' our dinner sweet.

Ye'll sit on his white hause-bane,
And I'll pike out his bonny blue e'en.
Wi' ae lock o' his gowden hair
We'll theek our nest when it grows bare.

Mony a one for him maks mane,
But nane sall ken whar he is gane.
O'er his white banes, when they are bare,
The wind sall blaw for evermair.'

ANON.

fail—turf.   *hause*—neck.   *theek*—thatch.

THE THREE RAVENS

There were three ravens sat on a tree,
They were as black as they might be.

The one of them said to his make,
'Where shall we our breakfast take?'

'Down in yonder greenè field
There lies a knight slain under his shield.

His hounds they lie down at his feet,
So well do they their master keep.

His hawks they fly so eagerly,
There's no fowl dare come him nigh.'

Down there comes a fallow doe
As great with young as she might goe.

She lift up his bloody head
And kist his wounds that were so red.

She gat him up upon her back
And carried him to earthen lake.

She buried him before the prime,
She was dead herself ere evensong time.

God send every gentleman
Such hounds, such hawks, and such a leman!

ANON.

The Twa Corbies is the Scottish, *The Three Ravens* the English version of the same theme. The Scottish ballads are, generally speaking, more stark and grim than the English. The bleak realism of the one is in striking contrast to the romantic pathos of the other. Which is the better poem?

EDWARD

'Why does your brand sae drop wi' blude,
  Edward, Edward?
Why does your brand sae drop wi' blude,
  And why sae sad gang ye, O?'
'O I hae kill'd my hawk sae gude,
  Mither, mither.
O I hae kill'd my hawk sae gude,
  And I had nae mair but he, O.'

'Your hawk's blude was never sae red,
  Edward, Edward.
Your hawk's blude was never sae red,
  My dear son, I tell thee, O.'
'O I hae kill'd my red-roan steed,
  Mither, mither.
O I hae kill'd my red-roan steed
  That erst was sae fair and free, O.'

'Your steed was auld, and ye hae got mair,
  Edward, Edward.
Your steed was auld, and ye hae got mair,
  Some other dule ye dree, O.'
'O I hae kill'd my father dear,
  Mither, mither.
O I hae kill'd my father dear,
  Alas and wae is me, O.'

'And whatten penance will ye dree for that,
  Edward, Edward?
Whatten penance will ye dree for that?
  My dear son, now tell me, O.'
'I'll set my feet on yonder boat,
  Mither, mither.
I'll set my feet on yonder boat,
  And I'll fare over the sea, O.'

'And what will ye do wi' your tow'rs and your ha',
  Edward, Edward?
And what will ye do wi' your tow'rs and your ha',
  That were sae fair to see, O?'
'I'll let them stand till they doun fa',
  Mither, mither.
I'll let them stand till they doun fa',
  For here never mair maun I be, O.'

'And what will ye leave to your bairns and your wife,
  Edward, Edward?
And what will ye leave to your bairns and your wife,
  When ye gang owre the sea, O?'
'The warld's room. Let them beg through life,
  Mither, mither.
The warld's room. Let them beg through life,
  For them never mair will I see, O.'

'And what will ye leave to your ain mither dear,
  Edward, Edward?
And what will ye leave to your ain mither dear,
  My dear son, now tell me, O?'
'The curse of hell frae me sall ye bear,
  Mither, mither.
The curse of hell frae me sall ye bear,
  Sic counsels ye gave to me, O!'

ANON.

A narrative poem is not always the straightforward telling of a story. This could be described as a 'dramatic lyric', constructed in the form of a highly patterned dialogue, the story developing to a tragic climax by means of the verse-pattern based upon the question and answer of mother and son. There are no explanations. The reason for the murder is left to the reader's imagination, and is all the more sinister. But there is ample material here for a novel or a tragic play.

THE DEATH OF NELSON

Come all gallant seamen that unite a meeting,
Attend to these lines that I'm going to relate
And, when that you hear, it will move you with pity
To hear how Lord Nelson, he met with his fate.
For he was a bold and undaunted commander
As ever did sail on the ocean wide,
And he made both the French and the Spaniards surrender
By always pouring into them a broadside.

Chorus

Mourn, England, mourn! Mourn and complain
For the loss of Lord Nelson, who died on the main.

From aloft to aloft, where he was commanding,
All by a French gun he received a ball
And by the contents he got mortally wounded
And that was the occasion of Lord Nelson's fall.
Like an undaunted hero, exposed to the fire
As he gave the command, on the quarter-deck stood,
And to hear of his actions, you would much admire,
To see the decks covered all with human blood.

One hundred engagements he had been into
And never, in his time, was he known to be beat,
For he had lost an arm, likewise his right eye, sir,
No powers on earth could ever him defeat.
His age at his death, it was forty and seven,
And as long as I live, his great praises I'll sing,
For the whole navigation was given unto him
Because he was loyal and true to his king.

Then up steps the doctor in a very great hurry
And unto Lord Nelson these words did he say,
Indeed then, my Lord, I am very sorry,
To see you lying and bleeding this way.
No matter, no matter whatever about me,
My time it has come, I'm almost at the worst,
And there's my gallant seamen who're fighting so boldly,
Go and discharge your duty to them first.

Then with a loud voice he called out to his captain,
Pray let me know how this battle does go,
I think that our guns continue to rattle,
Though death approaches I very well know.
The antagonist's ship has gone to the bottom,
Eighteen we've captured, and brought them on board,
And here are two of them quite blown out of the ocean,
So that is the news I have brought you, my Lord.

Come all gallant seamen that unite a meeting,
Always let Lord Nelson's memory go round;
For it is your duty when you unite a meeting,
Because he was loyal and true to the Crown.
So now to conclude and to finish these verses,
My time it is come, I am quite at the worst,
May the heavens go with you and ten thousand blessings
May rest in the Fleet with you, Lord Collingwood.

ANON.

Just as the old minstrel celebrated battles such as Otterburn and Chevy Chace
in ballads, so even in the early nineteenth century poems were written by
unknown versifiers to celebrate national events and were sung and sold in the
streets. The verse was crude and the syntax clumsy, but they often expressed
with an attractive naïveté the true sentiments of the man-in-the-street. This
ballad is an apt illustration of the common people's love of the great admiral
and their pride in the glory of his death. This is vividly described in Hardy's
The Dynasts from which *The Night of Trafalgar* (p. 151) is taken.

JOHN HENRY

John Henry was a lil baby,
Sittin' on his mama's knee,
Said, 'De Big Bend Tunnel on de C. & O. road
Gonna cause de death of me,
Lawd, lawd, gonna cause de death of me.'

Cap'n says to John Henry,
'Gonna bring me a steam drill 'round,
Gonna take dat steam drill out on de job,
Gonna whop dat steel on down,
Lawd, Lawd, gonna whop dat steel on down.'

John Henry tol' his cap'n,
Lightnin' was in his eye,
'Cap'n, bet yo' las' red cent on me,
Fo' I'll beat it to de bottom or I'll die,
Lawd, Lawd, I'll beat it to de bottom or I'll die.'

Sun shine hot an' burnin',
Weren't no breeze at all,
Sweat ran down like water down a hill,
Dat day John Henry let his hammer fall,
Lawd, Lawd, dat day John Henry let his hammer fall.

John Henry went to de tunnel,
An' dey put him in the lead to drive,
De rock so tall an' John Henry so small,
Dat he lied down his hammer an' he cried,
Lawd, Lawd, dat he lied down his hammer an' he cried.

John Henry started on de right hand,
De steam drill started on de lef'—
'Before I'd let dis steam drill beat me down,
I'd hammer my fool self to death,
Lawd, Lawd, I'd hammer my fool self to death.'

C. & O. road—Chesapeke and Ohio Railway.

White man tol' John Henry,
'Nigger, damn yo' soul,
You might beat dis steam and drill o' mine,
When de rocks in dis mountain turn to gol',
Lawd, Lawd, when de rocks in dis mountain turn to gol'.'

John Henry said to his shaker,
'Nigger, why don' you sing?
I'm throwin' twelve poun's from my hips on down,
Jes' listen to de col' steel ring,
Lawd, Lawd, jes' listen to de col' steel ring.'

Oh, de captain said to John Henry,
'I b'lieve this mountain's sinkin' in.'
John Henry said to his captain, oh my!
'Ain' nothin' but my hammer suckin' win',
Lawd, Lawd, ain' nothin' but my hammer suckin' win'.'

John Henry tol' his shaker,
'Shaker, you better pray,
For if I miss dis six-foot steel,
Tomorrow'll be yo' buryin' day,
Lawd, Lawd, tomorrow'll be yo' buryin' day.'

John Henry tol' his captain,
'Look yonder what I see—
Yo' drill's done broke an' yo' hole's done choke,
An' you cain drive steel like me,
Lawd, Lawd, an' you cain drive steel like me.'

De man dat invented de steam drill,
Thought he was mighty fine.
John Henry drove his fifteen feet,
An' de steam drill only made nine,
Lawd, Lawd, an' de steam drill only made nine.

---

shaker—work-mate. He held the steel drive steady for the hammer. John Henry had
to be accurate as well as fast, as one false blow could kill his 'shaker'.

De hammer dat John Henry swung,
It weighed over nine pound.
He broke a rib in his lef'-han' side,
An' his intrels fell on de groun',
Lawd, Lawd, an' his intrels fell on de groun'.

All de womens in de Wes',
When dey heared of John Henry's death,
Stood in de rain, flagged de eas'-boun' train,
Goin' where John Henry fell dead,
Lawd, Lawd, goin' where John Henry fell dead.

John Henry's lil mother,
She was all dressed in red,
She jumped in bed, covered up her head,
Said she didn' know her son was dead,
Lawd, Lawd, didn' know her son was dead.

Dey took John Henry to de graveyard,
An' dey buried him in de san',
An' every locomotive come roarin' by,
Says, 'Dere lays a steel-drivin' man,
Lawd, Lawd, dere lays a steel-drivin' man.'

ANON.

Although folk poetry petered out in Britain, it took on a new lease of life in the violent pioneering era of the expansion of the United States to the west. Ballads, spirituals and hill-billies were composed by the railway labourers, the negroes in the cotton fields and the cowboys on the ranches. This magnificent ballad comes from the railroad, and reveals something of the fierce and violent life of the railroad men in the era when railways were being pushed through undeveloped country and opening the way for settlers. Thousands of miles of lines were laid, bridges built and tunnels excavated through mountains, all by human labour until the introduction of mechanical excavators and plate-layers. The event narrated in this poem reveals not merely the resentment of the labourer at the introduction of mechanical aids, but, much more, his pride in his toughness and physical strength. Like the heroic poetry of old, this poem sings of great deeds of physical strength and of man's unconquerable spirit, driving the body to exhaustion and death. It is as terse, unsentimental and vivid as any of the old Border ballads.

Part Two

NARRATIVE POEMS

THE PARDONER'S TALE

In Flaundres whylom was a companye
Of yonge folk that haunteden folye,
As ryot, hasard, stewes and tavernes,
Wheras with harpes, lutes and giternes,
They daunce and pleye at dees bothe day and night,
And ete also and drinken over hir might,
Thurgh which they doon the devel sacrifyse
Within that develes temple, in cursed wyse,
By superfluitee abhominable.
Hir othes been so grete and so dampnable,   10
That it is grisly for to here hem swere;
Our blissed lordes body they to-tere;
Hem thoughte Jewes rente him noght y-nough;
And ech of hem at otheres sinne lough.

    .   .   .   .   .   .

Thise ryotoures three, of which I telle,
Longe erst er pryme rong of any belle,
Were set hem in a taverne for to drinke;
And as they satte, they herde a belle clinke
Biforn a cors, was caried to his grave.
That oon of hem gan callen to his knave,   20
'Go bet,' quod he, 'and axe redily,
What cors is this that passeth heer forby,
And look that thou reporte his name wel.'
'Sir,' quod this boy, 'it nedeth never-a-del.
It was me told, er ye cam heer, two houres.
He was, pardee, an old felawe of youres,
And sodeynly he was y-slayn tonight,

---

12 *to-tere*—tear to pieces. Lines 46 and 49 show how they swore by Christ's body.
16 *pryme*—the first hour of the day for the saying of the Divine Office—six a.m.

35

For-dronke, as he sat on his bench upright.
Ther cam a privee theef men clepeth Deeth,
That in this contree al the peple sleeth,   30
And with his spere he smoot his herte a-two,
And wente his wey withouten wordes mo.
He hath a thousand slayn this pestilence,
And, maister, er ye come in his presence,
Me thinketh that it were necessarie
For to be war of swich an adversarie;
Beth redy for to mete him evermore.
Thus taughte me my dame, I sey namore.'

'By seinte Marie,' seyde this taverner,
'The child seith sooth, for he hath slayn this yeer,   40
Henne over a myle, within a greet village,
Both man and womman, child and hyne and page.
I trowe his habitacioun be there.
To been avysed greet wisdom it were,
Er that he dide a man a dishonour,'
'Ye, goddes armes,' quod this ryotour,
'Is it swich peril with him for to mete?
I shal him seke by wey and eke by strete,
I make avow to goddes digne bones!
Herkneth, felawes, we three been al ones.   50
Lat ech of us holde up his hond til other,
And ech of us bicomen otheres brother,
And we wol sleen this false traytour Deeth.
He shal be slayn, which that so many sleeth,
By goddes dignitee, er it be night.'

Togidres han thise three her trouthes plight
To live and dyen ech of hem for other
As though he were his owene y-boren brother.

---

28 *for-dronke*—blind drunk. *Sat upright.* A drunken man would probably not sit upright. 'Sat' was used loosely in Chaucer's time, and 'upright' often meant 'lying on one's back'. Hence the drunken man was sprawling on his back.   42 *hyne*—peasant.

And up they sterte al dronken in this rage,
And forth they goon towardes that village   60
Of which the taverner had spoke biforn,
And many a grisly ooth than han they sworn,
And Cristes blessed body they to-rente—
'Deeth shal be deed, if that they may him hente.'

Whan they han goon nat fully half a myle,
Right as they wolde han troden over a style,
An old man and a povre with hem mette.
This olde man ful mekely hem grette
And seyde thus, 'Now lordes, god yow see!'
The proudest of thise ryotoures three   70
Answerde agayn, 'What! carl, with sory grace,
Why artow al forwrapped save thy face?
Why livestow so long in so greet age?'

This olde man gan loke in his visage,
And seyde thus, 'For I ne can nat finde
A man, though that I walked into Inde,
Neither in citee nor in no village,
That wolde chaunge his youthe for myn age;
And therfore moot I han my age stille
As longe time as it is goddes wille.   80
Ne deeth, allas, ne wol nat han my lyf.
Thus walke I, lyk a restelees caityf,
And on the ground, which is my modres gate,
I knokke with my staf, bothe erly and late,
And seye, "Leve moder, leet me in!
Lo, how I vanish, flesh, and blood, and skin!
Allas, whan shul my bones been at reste?
Moder, with yow wolde I chaunge my cheste,
That in my chambre longe tyme hath be,
Ye! for an heyre cloute to wrappe me!"   90

83 *modres*—mother's: mother is 'Mother Earth'. 85 *leve*—dear. 88 *cheste*—chest
(of clothes). 90 *heyre cloute*—a hair-cloth (for a shroud).

But yet to me she wol nat do that grace,
For which ful pale and welked is my face.
But, sirs, to yow it is no curteisye
To speken to an old man vileinye,
But he trespasse in worde or elles in dede.
In holy writ ye may yourself wel rede,
"Agayns an old man, hoor upon his heed,
Ye sholde aryse," wherfor I yeve yow reed,
Ne dooth unto an old man noon harm now,
Namore than ye wolde men dide to yow   100
In age, if that ye so longe abyde;
And god be with yow, wher ye go or ryde.
I moot go thider as I have to go.'

'Nay olde cherl, by god, thou shalt nat so,'
Seyde this other hasadour anon.
'Thou partest nat so lightly, by seint John!
Thou spak right now of thilke traitour Deeth,
That in this contree all our frendes sleeth.
Have heer my trouthe, as thou art his aspye,
Tel wher he is, or thou shalt it abye,   110
By god and by the holy sacrament!
For soothly thou art oon of his assent
To sleen us yonge folk, thou false theef!'

'Now, sirs,' quod he, 'if that yow be so leef
To finde Deeth, turne up this croked wey,
For in that grove I lafte him, by my fey,
Under a tree, and ther he wol abyde.
Nat for your boost he wol him nothing hyde.
See ye that ook? Right ther ye shul him finde.
God save yow, that boghte agayn mankinde,   120
And yow amende!' Thus seyde this olde man.

92 *welked*—withered.   98 *reed*—advice.   120 *boghte agayn*—redeemed.

And everich of thise ryotoures ran
Til he cam to that tree, and ther they founde
Of florins fyne of golde y-coyned rounde
Wel ny an eighte busshels, as hem thoughte.
No lenger thanne after Deeth they soughte,
But ech of hem so glad was of that sighte,
For that the florins been so faire and brighte,
That doun they sette hem by this precious hord.
The worste of hem he spak the firste word.   130
'Brethren,' quod he, 'tak kepe what I seye,
My wit is greet, though that I bourde and pleye.
This tresor hath fortune unto us yiven,
In mirthe and jolitee our lyf to liven,
And lightly as it comth, so wol we spende.
Ey! goddes precious dignitee! who wende
Today, that we sholde han so fair a grace?
But mighte this gold be caried fro this place
Hoom to myn hous or elles unto youres—
For wel ye woot that al this gold is oures—   140
Than were we in heigh felicitee.
But trewely by daye it may nat be;
Men wolde seyn that we were theves stronge,
And for our owene tresor doon us honge.
This tresor moste y-caried be by nighte
As wysly and as slyly as it mighte.
Wherfore I rede that cut among us alle
Be drawe and lat see wher the cut wol falle;
And he that hath the cut with herte blythe
Shal renne to the toune, and that ful swythe,   150
And bring us breed and wyn ful prively.
And two of us shul kepen subtilly
This tresor wel; and if he wol nat tarie,
Whan it is night, we wol this tresor carie
By oon assent wheras us thinketh best.'

128 *florin*—a gold coin, so-called because first minted in Florence.   132 *bourde*—jest.
150 *swythe*—quickly.

That oon of hem the cut broughte in his fest
And bad them drawe, and loke wher it wol falle.
And it fil on the yongeste of hem alle,
And forth toward the toun he wente anon.
And also sone as that he was gon,   160
That oon of hem spak thus unto that other,
'Thou knowest wel thou art my sworne brother,
Thy profit wol I telle thee anon.
Thou woost wel that our felawe is agon,
And heer is gold and that ful greet plentee
That shal departed been among us three.
But natheless, if I can shape it so
That it departed were among us two,
Hadde I nat doon a frendes torn to thee ?'
That other answerde, 'I noot how that may be.   170
He woot how that the gold is with us tweye.
What shal we doon, what shal we to him seye ?'
'Shal it be conseil ?' seyde the firste shrewe,
'And I shal tellen thee, in wordes fewe,
What shal we doon, and bringe it wel aboute.'
'I graunte,' quod that other, 'out of doute,
That, by my trouthe, I wol thee nat biwreye.'
'Now,' quod the firste, 'thou woost wel we be tweye,
And two of us shul strenger be than oon.
Look whan that he is set, and right anoon   180
Arys, as though thou woldest with him pleye,
And I shal ryve him thurgh the sydes tweye
Whyl that thou strogelest with him as in game,
And with thy dagger look thou do the same;
And than shal al this gold departed be,
My dere freend, bitwixen me and thee.
Than may we bothe our lustes al fulfille
And pleye at dees right at our owene wille.'
And thus acorded been thise shrewes tweye
To sleen the thridde, as ye han herd me seye.   190

166 *departed*—divided.   173 *shrewe*—scoundrel.

This yongest, which that wente unto the toun,
Ful ofte in herte he rolleth up and doun
The beautee of thise florins newe and brighte.
'O lorde!' quod he, 'if so were that I mighte
Have al this tresor to myself allone,
Ther is no man that liveth under the trone
Of god, that sholde live so mery as I!'
And atte laste the feend, our enemy,
Putte in his thought that he shold poyson beye
With which he mighte sleen his felawes tweye;   200
For-why the feend fond him in swich lyvinge
That he had leve him to sorwe bringe,
For this was outrely his fulle entente
To sleen hem bothe, and never to repente.
And forth he gooth, no lenger wolde he tarie,
Into the toun, unto a pothecarie,
And preyed him that he him wolde selle
Som poyson that he mighte his rattes quelle;
And eek ther was a polcat in his hawe
That, as he seyde, his capouns hadde y-slawe,   210
And fayn he wolde wreke him, if he mighte,
On vermin that destroyed him by nighte.

The pothecarie answerde, 'And thou shalt have
A thing that, also god my soule save,
In al this world ther nis no creature,
That ete or dronke hath of this confiture
Noght but the mountance of a corn of whete,
That he ne shal his lyf anon forlete;
Ye, sterve he shal, and that in lasse whyle
Than thou wolt goon a paas nat but a myle,   220
This poyson is so strong and violent.'

---

208 *quelle*—kill.   209 *hawe*—hedge.   219 *sterve*—die.   220 *goon a paas*—go apace, in
Chaucer's time, meaning 'at a walking pace'.

This cursed man hath in his hond y-hent
This poyson in a box, and sith he ran
Into the nexte strete unto a man
And borwed of him large botels three,
And in the two his poyson poured he.
The thridde he kepte clene for his drinke.
For al the night he shoop him for to swinke
In caryinge of the gold out of that place.
And whan this ryotour, with sory grace,   230
Had filled with wyn his grete botels three,
To his felawes agayn repaireth he.

What nedeth it to sermone of it more?
For right as they had cast his deeth bifore,
Right so they han him slayn, and that anon.
And whan that this was doon, thus spak that oon,
'Now lat us sitte and drinke and make us merie,
And afterward we wol his body berie.'
And with that word it happed him, par cas,
To take the botel ther the poyson was,   240
And drank and yaf his felawe drinke also,
For which anon they storven bothe two.

But, certes, I suppose that Avicen
Wroot never in no canon, ne in no fen,
Mo wonder signes of empoisoning
Than hadde thise wrecches two, er hir ending.
Thus ended been thise homicydes two,
And eek the false empoysoner also.

GEOFFREY CHAUCER

243 *Avicen*—Avicenna, a famous Arabian physician of the early eleventh century whose *Canon of Medicine* was a standard medical book, even in Chaucer's time. It was divided into Sections (Arabic *fen*).

Geoffrey Chaucer (1340-1400) was employed by the court on occasional diplomatic missions in France and Italy and held important posts at various times in Customs and Excise. The tale comes from *The Canterbury Tales*, which contains what have always been his most popular poems. In the *Prologue*, a brilliant pageant of medieval people, he tells how he joined a party of pilgrims setting out from the Tabard Inn in Southwark for a pilgrimage to Canterbury. The innkeeper decides to accompany them, and they agree with him to beguile the journey by telling tales, the best story to win the teller a free supper on their return to London.

The Pardoner, an itinerant preacher and seller of supposedly holy relics and 'pardons', and undoubtedly a quick-witted and plausible swindler (the pardoners were frequently denounced for their sharp practices and impostures), tells the company how he persuades simple people to part with their money by the eloquence of his sermons on the evils of cupidity. He is so moved by the power of his own tale that, forgetting that he has already exposed the tricks of his trade to the company, he tries them on the pilgrims in the hope that the moral of his story has gone home. His bare-faced impudence meets with an appropriate reply.

The story itself is not original, and, indeed, seems to be a very old one. One version is to be found in a collection of Buddhist stories called the *Jataka*, and another in *The Arabian Nights*. Chaucer may have taken it from a fourteenth-century Italian collection, *Cento Novelle Antiche* (A Hundred Old Stories). The story is impressive enough in the grim irony of its justice, but Chaucer's brilliant narrative power makes *The Pardoner's Tale* one of the finest short stories—and narrative poems—ever written.

The pestilence to which he refers in line 33 is one of the many outbreaks of plague which ravaged medieval Europe—probably the Great Plague of 1376. Death may well have seemed to be a sinister and terrible spirit stalking the land. Notice the skilful irony of the meeting of the three wastrels with the old man, a figure of great pathos. They seek Death to slay him so that they can live—but they die: he longs to die, and cannot. Much of the power of the story arises from Chaucer's skill in the selection of detail and observation, and in the increasing *tempo* of the narrative. He needs only nine lines to describe the terrible climax.

PETER GRIMES

Old Peter Grimes made fishing his employ,
His wife he cabin'd with him and his boy,
And seem'd that life laborious to enjoy:
To town came quiet Peter with his fish,
And had of all a civil word and wish.
He left his trade upon the sabbath-day,
And took young Peter in his hand to pray:
But soon the stubborn boy from care broke loose,
At first refused, then added his abuse:
His father's love he scorn'd, his power defied,   10
But being drunk, wept sorely when he died.

Yes! then he wept, and to his mind there came
Much of his conduct, and he felt the shame,—
How he had oft the good old man reviled,
And never paid the duty of a child;
How, when the father in his Bible read,
He in contempt and anger left the shed:
'It is the word of life,' the parent cried;
—'This is the life itself,' the boy replied;
And while old Peter in amazement stood,   20
Gave the hot spirit to his boiling blood:—
How he, with oath and furious speech, began
To prove his freedom and assert the man;
And when the parent check'd his impious rage,
How he had cursed the tyranny of age,—
Nay, once had dealt the sacrilegious blow
On his bare head, and laid his parent low;
The father groaned—'If thou art old,' said he,
'And hast a son—thou wilt remember me:
Thy mother left me in a happy time,   30
Thou kill'st not her—Heav'n spares the double crime.'

On an inn-settle, in his maudlin grief,
This he revolved, and drank for his relief.

Now lived the youth in freedom, but debarr'd
From constant pleasure, and he thought it hard;
Hard that he could not every wish obey,
But must awhile relinquish ale and play;
Hard that he could not to his cards attend,
But must acquire the money he would spend.

With greedy eye he look'd on all he saw,   40
He knew not justice, and he laugh'd at law;
On all he mark'd he stretched his ready hand;
He fish'd by water, and he filch'd by land:
Oft in the night has Peter dropp'd his oar,
Fled from his boat and sought for prey on shore;
Oft up the hedgerow glided, on his back
Bearing the orchard's produce in a sack,
Or farmyard load, tugg'd fiercely from the stack;
And as these wrongs to greater numbers rose,
The more he look'd on all men as his foes.   50

He built a mud-wall'd hovel, where he kept
His various wealth, and there he oft-times slept;
But no success could please his cruel soul,
He wish'd for one to trouble and control;
He wanted some obedient boy to stand
And bear the blows of his outrageous hand;
And hoped to find in some propitious hour
A feeling creature subject to his power.

Peter had heard there were in London then,—
Still have they being!—workhouse-clearing men,   60
Who, undisturb'd by feelings just or kind,
Would parish-boys to needy tradesmen bind:
They in their want a trifling sum would take,
And toiling slaves of piteous orphans make.

Such Peter sought, and when a lad was found,
The sum was dealt him, and the slave was bound.
Some few in town observed in Peter's trap
A boy, with jacket blue and woollen cap;
But none inquired how Peter used the rope,
Or what the bruise, that made the stripling stoop;   70
None could the ridges on his back behold,
None sought him shiv'ring in the winter's cold;
None put the question,—'Peter, dost thou give
The boy his food?—What, man, the lad must live:
Consider, Peter, let the child have bread,
He'll serve thee better if he's strok'd and fed.'
None reason'd thus—and some, on hearing cries,
Said calmly, 'Grimes is at his exercise.'

Pinn'd, beaten, cold, pinch'd, threaten'd, and abused—
His efforts punish'd, and his food refused,—   80
Awake tormented,—soon aroused from sleep,—
Struck if he wept, and yet compell'd to weep,
The trembling boy dropp'd down and strove to pray,
Received a blow, and trembling turn'd away,
Or sobb'd and hid his piteous face;—while he,
The savage master, grinn'd in horrid glee:
He'd now the power he ever loved to show,
A feeling being subject to his blow.

Thus liv'd the lad, in hunger, peril, pain,
His tears despised, his supplications vain: 90
Compell'd by fear to lie, by need to steal,
His bed uneasy and unbless'd his meal,
For three sad years the boy his tortures bore,
And then his pains and trials were no more.
'How died he, Peter?' when the people said,
He growl'd—'I found him lifeless in his bed';
Then tried for softer tone, and sigh'd, 'Poor Sam is dead.'

Yet murmurs were there, and some questions ask'd,—
How he was fed, how punish'd, and how task'd?
Much they suspected, but they little proved,   100
And Peter pass'd untroubled and unmoved.
Another boy with equal ease was found,
The money granted, and the victim bound;
And what his fate?—One night it chanced he fell
From the boat's mast and perish'd in her well,
Where fish were living kept, and where the boy
(So reason'd men) could not himself destroy:—
'Yes! so it was,' said Peter, 'in his play,
For he was idle both by night and day),
He climb'd the mainmast and then fell below';—   110
Then show'd his corpse and pointed to the blow:
'What said the jury?'—they were long in doubt,
But sturdy Peter faced the matter out:
So they dismiss'd him, saying at the time,
'Keep fast your hatchway when you've boys who climb.'
This hit the conscience, and he colour'd more
Than for the closest questions put before.

Thus all his fears the verdict set aside,
And at the slave-shop Peter still applied.

Then came a boy, of manners soft and mild,—   120
Our seamen's wives with grief beheld the child;
Passive he labour'd, till his slender frame
Bent with his loads, and he at length was lame:
Strange that a frame so weak could bear so long
The grossest insult and the foulest wrong;
But there were causes—in the town they gave
Fire, food, and comfort, to the gentle slave;
And though stern Peter, with a cruel hand,
And knotted rope, enforced the rude command,
Yet he consider'd what he'd lately felt,   130
And his vile blows with selfish pity dealt.

One day such draughts the cruel fisher made,
He could not vend them in his borough-trade,
But sail'd for London mart: the boy was ill,
But ever humbled to his master's will;
And on the river, where they smoothly sail'd,
He strove with terror and awhile prevail'd;
But new to danger on the angry sea,
He clung affrighted to his master's knee:
The boat grew leaky, and the wind was strong,   140
Rough was the passage and the time was long;
His liquor fail'd, and Peter's wrath arose,—
No more is known—the rest we must suppose,
Or learn of Peter;—Peter says, he 'spied
The stripling's danger and for harbour tried;
Meantime the fish, and then th' apprentice died.'
The pitying women raised a clamour round,
And weeping said, 'Thou hast thy 'prentice drown'd.'

Now the stern man was summon'd to the hall,
To tell his tale before the burghers all: 150
He gave th' account; profess'd the lad he loved,
And kept his brazen features all unmoved.
The mayor himself with tone severe replied,—
'Henceforth with thee shall never boy abide;
Hire thee a freeman, whom thou durst not beat,
But who, in thy despite, will sleep and eat:
Free art thou now!—again shouldst thou appear,
Thou'lt find thy sentence, like thy soul, severe.'

Alas! for Peter not a helping hand,
So was he hated, could he now command;   160
Alone he row'd his boat, alone he cast
His nets beside, or made his anchor fast;
To hold a rope or hear a curse was none,—
He toil'd and rail'd; he groan'd and swore alone.

Thus by himself compell'd to live each day,
To wait for certain hours the tide's delay;
At the same times the same dull views to see,
The bounding marsh-bank and the blighted tree;
The water only, when the tides were high,
When low, the mud half-cover'd and half-dry;   170
The sun-burnt tar that blisters on the planks
And bank-side stakes in their uneven ranks;
Heaps of entangled weeds that slowly float,
As the tide rolls by the impeded boat.

When tides were neap, and, in the sultry day,
Through the tall bounding mud-banks made their way,
Which on each side rose swelling, and below
The dark warm flood ran silently and slow;
There anchoring, Peter chose from man to hide,
There hang his head, and view the lazy tide   180
In its hot slimy channel slowly glide;
Where the small eels that left the deeper way
For the warm shore, within the shallows play;
Where gaping mussels, left upon the mud,
Slope their slow passage to the fallen flood;—
Here dull and hopeless he'd lie down and trace
How sidelong crabs had scrawl'd their crooked race;
Or sadly listen to the tuneless cry
Of fishing gull or clanging golden-eye;
What time the sea-birds to the marsh would come,   190
And the loud bittern, from the bull-rush home,
Gave from the salt-ditch side the bellowing boom:
He nursed the feelings these dull scenes produce,
And loved to stop beside the opening sluice;
Where the small stream, confined in narrow bound,
Ran with a dull, unvaried, sadd'ning sound;
Where all, presented to the eye or ear,
Oppress'd the soul with misery, grief and fear.

Besides these objects, there were places three,
Which Peter seem'd with certain dread to see;   200
When he drew near them he would turn from each,
And loudly whistle till he pass'd the reach.
A change of scene to him brought no relief;
In town, 'twas plain, men took him for a thief:
The sailors' wives would stop him in the street,
And say, 'Now, Peter, thou'st no boy to beat':
Infants at play, when they perceived him, ran,
Warning each other—'That's the wicked man':
He growl'd an oath, and in an angry tone
Cursed the whole place and wish'd to be alone.   210

Alone he was, the same dull scenes in view,
And still more gloomy in his sight they grew:
Though man he hated, yet employ'd alone
At bootless labour, he would swear and groan,
Cursing the shoals that glided by the spot,
And gulls that caught them when his arts could not.
Cold nervous tremblings shook his sturdy frame,
And strange disease—he couldn't say the name;
Wild were his dreams, and oft he rose in fright,
Waked by his view of horrors in the night,—   220
Horrors that would the sternest minds amaze,
Horrors that demons might be proud to raise:
And though he felt forsaken, grieved at heart,
To think he lived from all mankind apart;
Yet, if a man approach'd, in terror he would start.

A winter pass'd since Peter saw the town,
And summer-lodgers were again come down;
These, idly curious, with their glasses spied
The ships in bay as anchor'd for the tide,—
The river's craft,—the bustle of the quay,—   230
And sea-port views, which landmen love to see.

One, up the river, had a man and boat
Seen day by day, now anchor'd, now afloat;
Fisher he seem'd, yet used no net nor hook;
Of sea-fowl swimming by no heed he took,
But on the gliding waves still fix'd his lazy look:
At certain stations he would view the stream,
As if he stood bewilder'd in a dream,
Or that some power had chain'd him for a time,
To feel a curse or meditate on crime.   240

This known, some curious, some in pity went,
And others question'd—'Wretch, dost thou repent?'
He heard, he trembled, and in fear resign'd
His boat: new terror filled his restless mind;
Furious he grew, and up the country ran,
And there they seized him—a distemper'd man:—
Him we received, and to a parish-bed,
Follow'd and cursed, the groaning man was led.
Here when they saw him, whom they used to shun,
A lost, lone man, so harass'd and undone;   250
Our gentle females, ever prompt to feel,
Perceived compassion on their anger steal;
His crimes they could not from their memories blot,
But they were grieved, and trembled at his lot.
A priest too came, to whom his words are told;
And all the signs they shudder'd to behold.
'Look! look!' they cried; 'his limbs with horror shake,
And as he grinds his teeth, what noise they make!
How glare his angry eyes, and yet he's not awake:
See! what cold drops upon his forehead stand,   260
And how he clenches that broad bony hand.'

The priest attending, found he spoke at times
As one alluding to his fears and crimes:
'It was the fall,' he mutter'd, 'I can show
The manner how—I never struck a blow':—

And then aloud—'Unhand me, free my chain;
On oath, he fell—it struck him to the brain:—
Why ask my father ?—that old man will swear
Against my life; besides, he wasn't there:—
What, all agreed ?—Am I to die to-day ?—   270
My lord, in mercy, give me time to pray.'
Then, as they watch'd him, calmer he became,
And grew so weak he couldn't move his frame,
But murmuring spake,—while they could see and hear
The start of terror and the groan of fear;
See the large dew-beads on his forehead rise,
And the cold death-drop glaze his sunken eyes;
Nor yet he dies, but with unwonted force
Seem'd with some fancied being to discourse:
He knew not us, or with accustom'd art   280
He hid the knowledge, yet exposed his heart;
'Twas part confession and the rest defence,
A madman's tale, with gleams of waking sense.

'I'll tell you all,' he said, 'the very day
When the old man first placed them in my way:
My father's spirit—he who always tried
To give me trouble, when he lived and died—
When he was gone, he could not be content
To see my days in painful labour spent,
But would appoint his meetings, and he made   290
Me watch at these, and so neglect my trade.

' 'Twas one hot noon, all silent, still, serene,
No living being had I lately seen;
I paddled up and down and dipp'd my net,
But (such his pleasure) I could nothing get,—
A father's pleasure, when his toil was done,
To plague and torture thus an only son!
And so I sat and look'd upon the stream,
How it ran on, and felt as in a dream:

But dream it was not; no!—I fix'd my eyes 300
On the mid stream and saw the spirits rise;
I saw my father on the water stand,
And hold a thin pale boy in either hand;
And there they glided ghastly on the top
Of the salt flood, and never touch'd a drop:
I would have struck them, but they knew th' intent,
And smil'd upon the oar, and down they went.
Now, from that day, whenever I began
To dip my net, there stood the hard old man—
He and those boys: I humbled me and pray'd 310
They would be gone;—they heeded not, but stay'd:
Nor could I turn, nor would the boat go by,
But gazing on the spirits, there was I:
They bade me leap to death, but I was loth to die:
And every day, as sure as day arose,
Would these three spirits meet me ere the close;
To hear and mark them daily was my doom,
And "Come," they said, with weak, sad voices, "Come."
To row away with all my strength I try'd,
But there they were, hard by me in the tide, 320
The three unbodied forms—and "Come," still "Come" they
    cried.
'Fathers should pity—but this old man shook
His hoary locks, and froze me by a look:
Thrice, when I struck them, through the water came
A hollow groan, that weaken'd all my frame:
"Father!" said I, "have mercy":—He replied,
I know not what—the angry spirit lied,—
"Didst thou not draw thy knife?" said he:—'Twas true,
But I had pity and my arm withdrew:
He cried for mercy which I kindly gave, 330
But he has no compassion in his grave.
There were three places, where they ever rose,—
The whole long river had not such as those,—
Places accursed, where, if a man remain,

He'll see the things which strike him to the brain;
And there they made me on my paddle lean,
And look at them for hours;—accursed scene,
When they would glide to that smooth eddy-space,
Then bid me leap and join them in the place;
And at my groans each little villain sprite   340
Enjoy'd my pains, and vanish'd in delight.

'In one fierce summer-day, when my poor brain
Was burning hot and cruel was my pain,
Then came this father-foe, and there he stood
With his two boys again upon the flood;
There was more mischief in their eyes, more glee
In their pale faces when they glared at me:
And when they saw me fainting and oppress'd,
He, with his hand, the old man, scoop'd the flood,
And there came flame about him, mix'd with blood;   350
He bade me stoop, and look upon the place,
Then flung the hot-red liquor in my face;
Burning it blazed, and then I roar'd for pain,
I thought the demons would have turn'd my brain.
Still there they stood, and forced me to behold
A place of horrors—they cannot be told—
Where the flood open'd, there I heard the shriek
Of tortured guilt—no earthly tongue can speak:
"All days alike! for ever!" did they say,
"And unremitted torments every day"—   360
Yes, so they said': But here he ceased and gazed
On all around, affrighten'd and amazed;
And still he tried to speak, and look'd in dread
Of frighten'd females gathering round his bed;
Then dropp'd exhausted and appear'd at rest,
Till the strong foe the vital powers possess'd:
Then with an inward, broken voice he cried,
'Again they come,' and mutter'd as he died.

GEORGE CRABBE

George Crabbe (1754–1832) was born at Aldeburgh, a small and declining port on the Suffolk coast. After a long struggle against poverty and unhappiness as an unsuccessful apothecary, he attracted attention with his poems. He entered the Church and for the rest of his life was a parson in small country towns. His poems attracted considerable attention in his time. He turned from the charming, and rather sentimental, picture of village life and the countryside which had made Goldsmith's *Deserted Village* and *The Vicar of Wakefield* so popular, to paint a grim, realistic and rather disillusioned picture.

Peter Grimes is one of the stories from his longer poem *The Borough* (which is Aldeburgh). The story may strike us as melodramatic, but is supposed to be founded on truth. Indeed, it can hardly be accused of exaggeration, for Kingsley's *Water Babies* and Dickens's *Oliver Twist* reveal the cruel treatment afforded these unhappy foundling-apprentices long after Crabbe had written his story. *Peter Grimes* is realistic and does not aim at a superficial beauty. Its quality as narrative is enhanced by the hard matter-of-fact verse and by the power of concrete observation. A striking example of this is in the description of the mudbanks at low tide. Crabbe is particularly skilful in evoking atmosphere and the spirit of place, against which he places the guilt-haunted conscience of Grimes.

It is interesting that critics warned Crabbe against 'His frequent lapses into disgusting representations', and even suggested that the 'function of Poetry is not to present any truth if it is unpleasant'. But Byron described him as 'though Nature's sternest painter, yet the best'.

For many years Crabbe's poetry was regarded with distant respect and left in obscurity. But there has been, rightly, a revival of interest in this powerful narrative poet, a revival which has been quickened by the opera *Peter Grimes* by the English composer Benjamin Britten, who lives at Aldeburgh. The libretto of his opera is based on Crabbe's poem.

THE RIME OF THE ANCIENT MARINER

PART ONE

It is an ancient Mariner,
And he stoppeth one of three.
'By thy long grey beard and glittering eye,
Now wherefore stopp'st thou me?

An ancient Mariner meeteth three gallants bidden to a wedding feast, and detaineth one.

The Bridegroom's doors are opened wide,
And I am next of kin;
The guests are met, the feast is set;
May'st hear the merry din.'

He holds him with his skinny hand,
'There was a ship,' quoth he.
'Hold-off! unhand me, grey-beard loon!'
Eftsoons his hand dropt he.

He holds him with his glittering eye—
The Wedding-Guest stood still,
And listens like a three years' child:
The Mariner hath his will.

The Wedding-Guest is spellbound by the eye of the old seafaring man, and constrained to hear his tale.

The Wedding-Guest sat on a stone:
He cannot choose but hear;
And thus spake on that ancient man,
The bright-eyed Mariner.

'The ship was cheered, the harbour cleared,
Merrily did we drop
Below the kirk, below the hill,
Below the light-house top.

The sun came up upon the left,
Out of the sea came he!
And he shone bright, and on the right
Went down into the sea.

The Mariner tells how the ship sailed southward with a good wind and fair weather, till it reached the line.

Higher and higher every day,
Till over the mast at noon——,
The Wedding-Guest here beat his breast,
For he heard the loud bassoon.

The Bride hath paced into the hall,
Red as a rose is she;
Nodding their heads before her goes
The merry minstrelsy.

The Wedding-Guest heareth the bridal music; but the Mariner continueth his tale.

The Wedding-Guest he beat his breast,
Yet he cannot choose but hear;
And thus spake on that ancient man
The bright-eyed Mariner.

'And now the storm-blast came, and he
Was tyrannous and strong:
He struck with his o'ertaking wings,
And chased us south along.

The ship drawn by a storm toward the South Pole.

With sloping masts and dipping prow,
As who pursued with yell and blow
Still treads the shadow of his foe,
And forward bends his head,
The ship drove fast, loud roared the blast,
And southward aye we fled.

And now there came both mist and snow,
And it grew wondrous cold:
And ice, mast-high, came floating by,
As green as emerald.

And through the drifts the snowy clifts
Did send a dismal sheen:
Nor shapes of men nor beasts we ken—
The ice was all between.

The land of ice, and of fearful sounds, where no living thing was to be seen.

The ice was here, the ice was there,
The ice was all around:
It cracked and growled, and roared and howled,
Like noises in a swound!

At length did cross an Albatross,
Through the fog it came;
As if it had been a Christian soul,
We hailed it in God's name.

Till a great sea-bird called the Albatross came through the snow-fog, and was received with great joy and hospitality.

It ate the food it ne'er had eat,
And round and round it flew.
The ice did split with a thunder-fit;
The helmsman steered us through!

And a good south wind sprung up behind;
The Albatross did follow,
And every day, for food or play,
Came to the mariners' hollo!

And lo! the Albatross proveth a bird of good omen, and followeth the ship as it returned northward through fog and floating ice.

In mist or cloud, on mast or shroud,
It perched for vespers nine;
Whiles all the night, through fog-smoke white
Glimmered the white moon-shine.'

'God save thee, ancient Mariner,
From the fiends, that plague thee thus!—
Why look'st thou so?'—'With my cross-bow
I shot the Albatross.'

The ancient Mariner inhospitably killeth the pious bird of good omen.

PART TWO

'The Sun now rose upon the right:
Out of the sea came he,
Still hid in mist, and on the left
Went down into the sea.

And the good south wind still blew behind,
But no sweet bird did follow,
Nor any day for food or play
Came to the mariners' hollo!

And I had done a hellish thing,
And it would work 'em woe:
For all averred, I had killed the bird
That made the breeze to blow.
Ah wretch! said they, the bird to slay,
That made the breeze to blow!

His shipmates cry out against the ancient Mariner, for killing the bird of good luck.

Nor dim nor red, like God's own head,
The glorious Sun uprist:
Then all averred, I had killed the bird
That brought the fog and mist.
'Twas right, said they, such birds to slay,
That bring the fog and mist.

But when the fog cleared off, they justify the same, and thus make themselves accomplices in the crime.

The fair breeze blew, the white foam flew,
The furrow follow'd free;
We were the first that ever burst
Into that silent sea.

The fair breeze continues; the ship enters the Pacific Ocean, and sails northward, even till it reaches the Line.

Down dropt the breeze, the sails dropt down,
'Twas sad as sad could be;
And we did speak only to break
The silence of the sea!

The ship hath been suddenly becalmed.

All in a hot and copper sky,
The bloody Sun, at noon,
Right above the mast did stand,
No bigger than the Moon.

Day after day, day after day,
We stuck, nor breath nor motion;
As idle as a painted ship
Upon a painted ocean.

Water, water, everywhere,
And all the boards did shrink;
Water, water, everywhere,
Nor any drop to drink.

And the Albatross begins to be avenged.

The very deep did rot: O Christ!
That ever this should be!
Yea, slimy things did crawl with legs
Upon the slimy sea.

About, about, in reel and rout
The death-fires danced at night;
The water, like a witch's oils,
Burnt green, and blue, and white.

A Spirit had followed them; one of the invisible inhabitants of this planet, neither departed souls nor angels; concerning whom the learned Jew, Josephus, and the Platonic Constantinopolitan, Michael Psellus, may be consulted. They are very numerous, and there is no climate or element without one or more.

And some in dreams assurèd were
Of the Spirit that plagued us so;
Nine fathom deep he had followed us
From the land of mist and snow.

And every tongue, through utter drought,
Was withered at the root;
We could not speak, no more than if
We had been choked with soot.

The shipmates in their sore distress, would fain throw the whole guilt on

Ah! well a-day! what evil looks
Had I from old and young!
Instead of the cross, the Albatross
About my neck was hung.'

the ancient Mariner;
in sign whereof they
hang the dead sea-
bird round his neck.

PART THREE

'There passed a weary time.   Each throat
Was parched, and glazed each eye.
A weary time! a weary time!
How glazed each weary eye!
When looking westward, I beheld
A something in the sky.

The ancient Mari-
ner beholdeth a sign
in the element afar
off.

At first it seemed a little speck,
And then it seemed a mist;
It moved and moved, and took at last
A certain shape, I wist.

A speck, a mist, a shape, I wist!
And still it neared and neared:
As if it dodged a water-sprite,
It plunged, and tacked, and veered.

With throats unslaked, with black lips baked,
We could nor laugh nor wail;
Through utter drought all dumb we stood!
I bit my arm, I sucked the blood,
And cried, "A sail! a sail!"

At its nearer ap-
proach, it seemeth
him to be a ship;
and at a dear ransom
he freeth his speech
from the bonds of
thirst.

With throats unslaked, with black lips baked,
Agape they heard me call:
Gramercy! they for joy did grin,
And all at once their breath drew in,
As they were drinking all.

A flash of joy!

"See! see!" (I cried) "she tacks no more!
Hither to work us weal—
Without a breeze, without a tide,
She steadies with upright keel!"

And horror follows. For can it be a ship that comes onward without wind or tide?

The western wave was all aflame,
The day was wellnigh done!
Almost upon the western wave
Rested the broad, bright Sun;
When that strange shape drove suddenly
Betwixt us and the Sun.

And straight the Sun was flecked with bars
(Heaven's Mother send us grace!),
As if through a dungeon-grate he peered
With broad and burning face.

It seemeth him but the skeleton of a ship.

Alas! (thought I, and my heart beat loud)
How fast she nears and nears!
Are those her sails that glance in the Sun,
Like restless gossameres?

Are those her ribs through which the Sun
Did peer, as through a grate?
And is that Woman all her crew?
Is that a Death? and are there two?
Is Death that Woman's mate?

And its ribs are seen as bars on the face of the setting Sun. The Spectre-Woman and her Death-mate, and no other, on board the skeleton ship. Like vessel like crew!

Her lips were red, her looks were free,
Her locks were yellow as gold:
Her skin was as white as leprosy,
The Nightmare Life-in-Death was she,
Who thicks man's blood with cold.

The naked hulk alongside came,
And the twain were casting dice;
"The game is done! I've won! I've won!"
Quoth she, and whistles thrice.

Death and Life-in-Death have diced for the ship's crew, and she (the latter) winneth the ancient Mariner.

The Sun's rim dips; the stars rush out:
At one stride comes the dark;
With far-heard whisper, o'er the sea,
Off shot the spectre-bark.

No twilight within the courts of the Sun.

We listened and looked sideways up!
Fear at my heart, as at a cup,
My life-blood seem'd to sip!
The stars were dim, and thick the night,
The steersman's face by his lamp gleamed
    white;
From the sails the dew did drip—
Till clomb above the eastern bar
The hornèd Moon, with one bright star
Within the nether tip.

At the rising of the Moon,

One after one, by the star-dogged Moon,
Too quick for groan or sigh,
Each turned his face with a ghastly pang,
And cursed me with his eye.

One after another,

Four times fifty living men
(And I heard nor sigh nor groan),
With heavy thump, a lifeless lump,
They dropp'd down one by one.

His shipmates drop down dead.

The souls did from their bodies fly—
They fled to bliss or woe!
And every soul, it passed me by
Like the whizz of my crossbow!'

But Life-in-Death begins her work on the ancient Mariner.

PART FOUR

'I fear thee, ancient Mariner!
I fear thy skinny hand!
And thou art long, and lank, and brown,
As is the ribbed sea-sand.

The Wedding-Guest feareth that a Spirit is talking to him.

I fear thee and thy glittering eye,
And thy skinny hand, so brown.'—
'Fear not, fear not, thou Wedding-Guest!
This body dropt not down.

But the ancient Mariner assureth him of his bodily life, and proceedeth to relate his horrible penance.

Alone, alone, all, all alone,
Alone on a wide, wide sea!
And never a saint took pity on
My soul in agony.

The many men, so beautiful!
And they all dead did lie:
And a thousand thousand slimy things
Lived on: and so did I.

He despiseth the creatures of the calm.

I looked upon the rotting sea,
And drew my eyes away;
I looked upon the rotting deck,
And there the dead men lay.

And envieth that they should live, and so many lie dead.

I looked to Heaven, and tried to pray;
But or ever a prayer had gusht,
A wicked whisper came, and made
My heart as dry as dust.

I closed my lids, and kept them close,
And the balls like pulses beat;
For the sky and the sea, and the sea and the sky,
Lay like a load on my weary eye,
And the dead were at my feet.

The cold sweat melted from their limbs,
Nor rot nor reek did they:
The look with which they looked on me
Had never passed away.

But the curse liveth for him in the eye of the dead men.

An orphan's curse would drag to hell
A spirit from on high;
But oh! more horrible than that
Is a curse in a dead man's eye!
Seven days, seven nights, I saw that curse,
And yet I could not die.

The moving Moon went up the sky,
And nowhere did abide;
Softly she was going up,
And a star or two beside—

In his loneliness and fixedness he yearneth towards the journeying Moon, and the stars that still sojourn, yet still move onward; and everywhere the blue sky belongs to them, and is their appointed rest, and their native country, and their own natural homes, which they enter unannounced, as lords that are certainly expected, and yet there is a silent joy at their arrival.

Her beams bemocked the sultry main,
Like April hoar-frost spread;
But where the ship's huge shadow lay,
The charmèd water burned alway
A still and awful red.

Beyond the shadow of the ship,
I watched the water-snakes:
They moved in tracks of shining white,
And when they reared, the elfish light
Fell off in hoary flakes.

By the light of the Moon he beholdeth God's creatures of the great calm.

Within the shadow of the ship
I watched their rich attire:
Blue, glossy green, and velvet black,
They coiled and swam; and every track
Was a flash of golden fire.

O happy living things! no tongue
Their beauty might declare:
A spring of love gushed from my heart,
And I blessed them unaware:
Sure my kind saint took pity on me,
And I blessed them unaware.

Their beauty and their happiness.

He blesseth them in his heart.

The selfsame moment I could pray;
And from my neck so free
The Albatross fell off, and sank
Like lead into the sea.'

The spell begins to break.

Part Five

'O sleep! it is a gentle thing,
Beloved from pole to pole!
To Mary Queen the praise be given!
She sent the gentle sleep from Heaven,
That slid into my soul.

The silly buckets on the deck,
That had so long remained,
I dreamt that they were filled with dew;
And when I awoke, it rained.

By the grace of the holy Mother, the ancient Mariner is refreshed with rain.

My lips were wet, my throat was cold,
My garments all were dank;
Sure I had drunken in my dreams,
And still my body drank.

I moved, and could not feel my limbs:
I was so light—almost
I thought that I had died in sleep,
And was a blessèd ghost.

And soon I heard a roaring wind:
It did not come anear;
But with its sound it shook the sails,
That were so thin and sere.

He heareth sounds and seeth strange sights and commotions in the sky and the element.

The upper air burst into life;
And a hundred fire-flags sheen;
To and fro they were hurried about!
And to and fro, and in and out,
The wan stars danced between.

And the coming wind did roar more loud,
And the sails did sigh like sedge;
And the rain pour'd down from one black
    cloud;
The Moon was at its edge.

The thick black cloud was cleft, and still
The Moon was at its side;
Like waters shot from some high crag,
The lightning fell with never a jag,
A river steep and wide.

The loud wind never reached the ship,
Yet now the ship moved on!
Beneath the lightning and the Moon
The dead men gave a groan.

The bodies of the ship's crew are inspired, and the ship moves on.

They groaned, they stirred, they all uprose,
Nor spake, nor moved their eyes;
It had been strange, even in a dream,
To have seen those dead men rise.

The helmsman steered, the ship moved on;
Yet never a breeze up-blew;
The mariners all 'gan work the ropes,
Where they were wont to do;
They raised their limbs like lifeless tools—
We were a ghastly crew.

The body of my brother's son
Stood by me, knee to knee:
The body and I pull'd at one rope,
But he said naught to me.'

'I fear thee, ancient Mariner!'
'Be calm, thou Wedding-Guest:
'Twas not those souls that fled in pain,
Which to their corses came again,
But a troop of spirits blest:

But not by the souls of the men, nor by demons of earth or middle air, but by a blessed troop of angelic spirits, sent down by the invocation of the guardian saint.

For when it dawn'd—they dropped their arms,
And clustered round the mast;
Sweet sounds rose slowly through their
    mouths,
And from their bodies passed.

Around, around, flew each sweet sound,
Then darted to the Sun;
Slowly the sounds came back again,
Now mixed, now one by one.

Sometimes a-dropping from the sky
I heard the skylark sing;
Sometimes all little birds that are,
How they seemed to fill the sea and air
With their sweet jargoning!

And now 'twas like all instruments,
Now like a lonely flute;
And now it is an angel's song,
That makes the Heavens be mute.

It ceased; yet still the sails made on
A pleasant noise till noon,
A noise like of a hidden brook
In the leafy month of June,
That to the sleeping woods all night
Singeth a quiet tune.

Till noon we quietly sailed on,
Yet never a breeze did breathe:
Slowly and smoothly went the ship,
Moved onward from beneath.

Under the keel nine fathom deep,
From the land of mist and snow,
The Spirit slid: and it was he
That made the ship to go.
The sails at noon left off their tune,
And the ship stood still also.

The lonesome Spirit from the South Pole carries on the ship as far as the Line, in obedience to the angelic troop, but still requireth vengeance.

The Sun, right up above the mast,
Had fixed her to the ocean:
But in a minute she 'gan stir,
With a short uneasy motion—
Backwards and forwards half her length
With a short uneasy motion.

Then like a pawing horse let go,
She made a sudden bound:
It flung the blood into my head,
And I fell down in a swound.

How long in that same fit I lay,
I have not to declare;
But ere my living life returned
I heard, and in my soul discerned
Two voices in the air.

The Polar Spirit's fellow-demons, the invisible inhabitants of the element, take part in his wrong; and two of them relate, one to the other, that penance long and heavy for the ancient Mariner hath been accorded to the Polar Spirit, who returneth southward.

"Is it he?" quoth one, "is this the man?
By Him who died on cross,
With his cruel blow he laid full low
The harmless Albatross.

The Spirit who bideth by himself
In the land of mist and snow,
He loved the bird that loved the man
Who shot him with his bow."

The other was a softer voice,
As soft as honey-dew:
Quoth he, "The man hath penance done,
And penance more will do." '

PART SIX

First Voice:
' "But tell me, tell me! speak again,
Thy soft response renewing—
What makes that ship drive on so fast?
What is the Ocean doing?"

Second Voice:
"Still as a slave before his lord,
The Ocean hath no blast;
His great bright eye most silently
Up to the Moon is cast—

If he may know which way to go;
For she guides him smooth or grim.
See, brother, see! how graciously
She looketh down on him."

First Voice:
"But why drives on that ship so fast,
Without or wave or wind?"

The Mariner hath been cast into a trance; for the angelic power causeth the vessel to drive northward faster than human life could endure.

Second Voice:
"The air is cut away before,
And closes from behind.

Fly, brother, fly! more high, more high!
Or we shall be belated:
For slow and slow that ship will go,
When the Mariner's trance is abated."

I woke, and we were sailing on
As in a gentle weather:
'Twas night, calm night, the Moon was high;
The dead men stood together.

The supernatural motion is retarded; the Mariner awakes, and his penance begins anew.

All stood together on the deck,
For a charnel-dungeon fitter:
All fixed on me their stony eyes,
That in the Moon did glitter.

The pang, the curse, with which they died,
Had never passed away:
I could not draw my eyes from theirs,
Nor turn them up to pray.

And now this spell was snapt: once more   The curse is finally
I viewed the ocean green,   expiated.
And look'd far forth, yet little saw
Of what had else been seen—

Like one that on a lonesome road
Doth walk in fear and dread,
And having once turned round, walks on,
And turns no more his head;
Because he knows a frightful fiend
Doth close behind him tread.

But soon there breathed a wind on me,
Nor sound nor motion made:
Its path was not upon the sea,
In ripple or in shade.

It raised my hair, it fanned my cheek
Like a meadow-gale of spring—
It mingled strangely with my fears,
Yet it felt like a welcoming.

Swiftly, swiftly flew the ship,
Yet she sailed softly too:
Sweetly, sweetly blew the breeze—
On me alone it blew.

O dream of joy! is this indeed
The lighthouse top I see?
Is this the hill, is this the kirk
Is this mine own countree?

And the ancient
Mariner beholdeth
his native country.

We drifted o'er the harbour-bar,
And I with sobs did pray—
O let me be awake, my God!
Or let me sleep alway.

The harbour-bay was clear as glass,
So smoothly it was strewn!
And on the bay the moonlight lay,
And the shadow of the Moon.

The rock shone bright, the kirk no less
That stands above the rock:
The moonlight steeped in silentness
The steady weathercock.

And the bay was white with silent light
Till rising from the same,
Full many shapes, that shadows were,
In crimson colours came.

The angelic
spirits leave the
dead bodies;

A little distance from the prow
Those crimson shadows were:
I turned my eyes upon the deck—
O Christ! what saw I there!

And appear in
their own forms of
light.

Each corse lay flat, lifeless and flat,
And, by the holy rood!
A man all light, a seraph-man,
On every corse there stood.

This seraph-band, each waved his hand:
It was a heavenly sight!
They stood as signals to the land,
Each one a lovely light;

This seraph-band, each waved his hand,
No voice did they impart—
No voice; but oh! the silence sank
Like music on my heart.

But soon I heard the dash of oars,
I heard the Pilot's cheer;
My head was turned perforce away,
And I saw a boat appear.

The Pilot and the Pilot's boy,
I heard them coming fast:
Dear Lord in Heaven! it was a joy
The dead men could not blast.

I saw a third—I heard his voice:
It is the Hermit good!
He singeth loud his godly hymns
That he makes in the wood.
He'll shrieve my soul, he'll wash away
The Albatross's blood.'

PART SEVEN

'This hermit good lives in that wood
Which slopes down to the sea.
How loudly his sweet voice he rears!
He loves to talk with marineres
That come from a far countree.

The Hermit of
the wood.

He kneels at morn, and noon, and eve—
He hath a cushion plump:
It is the moss that wholly hides
The rotted old oak-stump.

The skiff-boat neared: I heard them talk,
"Why, this is strange, I trow!
Where are those lights so many and fair,
That signal made but now?"

"Strange, by my faith!" the Hermit said—   Approacheth the
"And they answered not our cheer!   ship with wonder.
The planks look warped! and see those sails,
How thin they are and sere!
I never saw aught like to them,
Unless perchance it were

Brown skeletons of leaves that lag
My forest-brook along;
When the ivy-tod is heavy with snow,
And the owlet whoops to the wolf below,
That eats the she-wolf's young."

"Dear Lord! it hath a fiendish look—
(The Pilot made reply)
I am a-feared"—"Push on, push on!"
Said the Hermit cheerily.

The boat came closer to the ship,
But I nor spake nor stirred;
The boat came close beneath the ship,
And straight a sound was heard.

Under the water it rumbled on,   The ship suddenly
sinketh.
Still louder and more dread:
It reached the ship, it split the bay;
The ship went down like lead.

Stunned by that loud and dreadful sound,   The ancient Mari-
ner is saved in the
Pilot's boat.
Which sky and ocean smote,
Like one that hath been seven days drowned
My body lay afloat;
But swift as dreams, myself I found
Within the Pilot's boat.

Upon the whirl, where sank the ship,
The boat spun round and round;
And all was still, save that the hill
Was telling of the sound.

I moved my lips—the Pilot shrieked
And fell down in a fit;
The holy Hermit raised his eyes,
And prayed where he did sit.

I took the oars: the Pilot's boy,
Who now doth crazy go,
Laughed loud and long, and all the while
His eyes went to and fro.
"Ha! ha!" quoth he, "full plain I see,
The Devil knows how to row."

And now, all in my own countree,
I stood on the firm land!
The Hermit stepped forth from the boat,
And scarcely he could stand.

"O shrieve me, shrieve me, holy man!"
The Hermit crossed his brow.
"Say quick," quoth he, "I bid thee say—
What manner of man art thou?"

The ancient Mariner earnestly entreateth the Hermit to shrive him; and the penance of life falls on him.

Forthwith this frame of mine was wrenched
With a woeful agony,
Which forced me to begin my tale;
And then it left me free.

Since then, at an uncertain hour,
That agony returns:
And till my ghastly tale is told,
This heart within me burns.

And ever and anon throughout his future life an agony constraineth him to travel from land to land.

I pass, like night, from land to land;
I have strange power of speech;
That moment that his face I see,
I know the man that must hear me:
To him my tale I teach.

What loud uproar bursts from that door!
The wedding-guests are there:
But in the garden-bower the Bride
And Bride-maids singing are:
And hark the little vesper bell,
Which biddeth me to prayer!

O Wedding-Guest! this soul hath been
Alone on a wide, wide sea:
So lonely 'twas, that God Himself
Scarce seemèd there to be.

O sweeter than the marriage-feast,
'Tis sweeter far to me,
To walk together to the kirk
With a goodly company!—

To walk together to the kirk,
And all together pray,
While each to his great Father bends,
Old men, and babes, and loving friends,
And youths and maidens gay!

Farewell, farewell, but this I tell
To thee, thou Wedding-Guest!
He prayeth well, who loveth well
Both man, and bird, and beast.

And to teach, by his own example, love and reverence to all things that God made and loveth.

He prayeth best, who loveth best
All things both great and small;
For the dear God who loveth us,
He made and loveth all.'

The Mariner, whose eye is bright,
Whose beard with age is hoar,
Is gone: and now the Wedding-Guest
Turned from the Bridegroom's door.

He went like one that hath been stunned,
And is of sense forlorn:
A sadder and a wiser man,
He rose the morrow morn.

S. T. COLERIDGE

Samuel Taylor Coleridge (1772–1834), poet, critic and philosopher, collaborated with his friend William Wordsworth in *Lyrical Ballads* (1798), to which he contributed *The Rime of the Ancient Mariner*. This volume, in its themes and style, marked an important break with the poetry of the earlier part of the century. Coleridge writes thus of what he and Wordsworth were trying to do in this remarkable volume:

During the first year that Mr. Wordsworth and I were neighbours, our conversations turned frequently on the two cardinal points of poetry, the power of exciting the sympathy of the reader by a faithful adherence to the truth of nature, and the power of giving the interest of novelty by the modifying colors of the imagination. The sudden charm, which accidents of light and shade, which moonlight or sun-set diffused over a known and familiar landscape, appeared to represent the practicability of combining both. These are the poetry of nature. The thought suggested itself (to which of us I do not recollect) that a series of poems might be composed of two sorts. In the one, the incidents and agents were to be, in part at least, super-natural; and the excellence aimed at was to consist in the interesting of the affections by the dramatic truth of such emotions, as would naturally accompany such situations, supposing them real. And real in *this* sense they have been to every human being who, from whatever source of delusion, has at any time believed himself under supernatural agency. For the second class, subjects were to be chosen from ordinary life; the characters and incidents were to be such, as will be found in every village and its vicinity, where there is a meditative and feeling mind to seek after them, or to notice them, when they present themselves.

Coleridge's contribution was of the first kind. Notice how subtly he leads us into an acceptance of the supernatural. After the first strange compulsion imposed by the mariner upon the wedding-guest, we have a simple narration of a voyage which is, at first, ordinary and commonplace. The tension increases in Part Two, but the events so colourfully described are still within the limits of the natural. We are thus led on to accept the terror of the super-natural and to accept it imaginatively all the more readily because of the vivid sensuousness of the imagery.

The conclusion has been criticised for its rather obvious moral and for the weakening of the poetic tension, but this criticism is hardly fair. Just as after the climax of a Shakespearian tragedy we are brought back to order and ordi-nariness, so Coleridge brings the mariner, the wedding-guest and the reader back to ordinary life, deepened by the spiritual tragedy and profoundly spiritual triumph of the mariner's experience.

MICHAEL

If from the public way you turn your steps
Up the tumultuous brook of Green-head Ghyll,
You will suppose that with an upright path
Your feet must struggle; in such bold ascent
The pastoral mountains front you, face to face.
But courage! for around that boisterous brook
The mountains have all opened out themselves,
And made a hidden valley of their own.
No habitation can be seen; but they
Who journey thither find themselves alone   10
With a few sheep, with rocks and stones, and kites
That overhead are sailing in the sky.
It is in truth an utter solitude;
Nor should I have made mention of this Dell
But for one object which you might pass by,
Might see and notice not. Beside the brook
Appears a straggling heap of unhewn stones!
And to that simple object appertains
A story—unenriched with strange events,
Yet not unfit, I deem, for the fireside,   20
Or for the summer shade. It was the first
Of those domestic tales that spake to me
Of Shepherds, dwellers in the valleys, men
Whom I already loved;—not verily
For their own sakes, but for the fields and hills
Where was their occupation and abode.
And hence this Tale, while I was yet a Boy
Careless of books, yet having felt the power
Of Nature, by the gentle agency

11 *kite*—a bird of prey and carrion, once common in England.

Of natural objects, led me on to feel   30
For passions that were not my own, and think
(At random and imperfectly indeed)
On man, the heart of man, and human life.
Therefore, although it be a history
Homely and rude, I will relate the same
For the delight of a few natural hearts;
And, with yet fonder feeling, for the sake
Of youthful Poets, who among these hills
Will be my second self when I am gone.

Upon the forest-side in Grasmere Vale   40
There dwelt a Shepherd, Michael was his name;
An old man, stout of heart, and strong of limb.
His bodily frame had been from youth to age
Of an unusual strength: his mind was keen,
Intense and frugal, apt for all affairs,
And in his shepherd's calling he was prompt
And watchful more than ordinary men.
Hence he had learned the meaning of all winds,
Of blasts of every tone; and oftentimes,
When others heeded not, he heard the South   50
Make subterraneous music, like the noise
Of bagpipers on distant Highland hills.
The Shepherd, at such warning, of his flock
Bethought him, and he to himself would say,
'The winds are now devising work for me!'
And, truly, at all times, the storm, that drives
The traveller to a shelter, summoned him
Up to the mountains: he had been alone
Amid the heart of many thousand mists,
That came to him, and left him, on the heights.   60
So lived he till his eightieth year was past.
And grossly that man errs, who should suppose
That the green valleys, and the streams and rocks,

Were things indifferent to the Shepherd's thoughts.
Fields, where with cheerful spirits he had breathed
The common air; hills, which with vigorous step
He had so often climbed; which had impressed
So many incidents upon his mind
Of hardship, skill or courage, joy or fear;
Which, like a book, preserved the memory   70
Of the dumb animals, whom he had saved,
Had fed or sheltered, linking to such acts
The certainty of honourable gain;
Those fields, those hills—what could they less? had laid
Strong hold on his affections, were to him
A pleasurable feeling of blind love,
The pleasure which there is in life itself.

His days had not been passed in singleness.
His Helpmate was a comely matron, old—
Though younger than himself full twenty years.   80
She was a woman of a stirring life,
Whose heart was in her house: two wheels she had
Of antique form; this large, for spinning wool;
That small, for flax; and, if one wheel had rest,
It was because the other was at work.
The Pair had but one inmate in their house,
An only Child, who had been born to them
When Michael, telling o'er his years, began
To deem that he was old,—in shepherd's phrase,
With one foot in the grave. This only Son,   90
With two brave sheep-dogs tried in many a storm,
The one of an inestimable worth,
Made all their household. I may truly say,
That they were as a proverb in the vale
For endless industry. When day was gone,
And from their occupations out of doors
The Son and Father were come home, even then,
Their labour did not cease; unless when all

Turned to the cleanly supper-board, and there,
Each with a mess of pottage and skimmed milk, 100
Sat round the basket piled with oaten cakes,
And their plain home-made cheese. Yet when the meal
Was ended, Luke (for so the Son was named)
And his old Father both betook themselves
To such convenient work as might employ
Their hands by the fire-side; perhaps to card
Wool for the Housewife's spindle, or repair
Some injury done to sickle, flail or scythe,
Or other implement of house or field.
Down from the ceiling, by the chimney's edge, 110
That in our ancient uncouth country style
With huge and black projection overbrowed
Large space beneath, as duly as the light
Of day grew dim the Housewife hung a lamp;
An aged utensil, which had performed
Service beyond all others of its kind.
Early at evening did it burn—and late,
Surviving comrade of uncounted hours,
Which, going by from year to year, had found,
And left, the couple neither gay perhaps 120
Nor cheerful, yet with objects and with hopes,
Living a life of eager industry.
And now, when Luke had reached his eighteenth year,
There by the light of this old lamp they sate,
Father and Son, while far into the night
The Housewife plied her own peculiar work,
Making the cottage through the silent hours
Murmur as with the sound of summer flies.
This light was famous in its neighbourhood,
And was a public symbol of the life 130
The thrifty Pair had lived. For, as it chanced,
Their cottage on a plot of rising ground
Stood single, with large prospect, north and south,
High into Easedale, up to Dunmail-Raise,

And westward to the village near the lake;
And from this constant light, so regular,
And so far seen, the House itself, by all
Who dwelt within the limits of the vale,
Both old and young, was named THE EVENING STAR.

Thus living on through such a length of years,   140
The Shepherd, if he loved himself, must needs
Have loved his Helpmate; but to Michael's heart
This son of his old age was yet more dear—
Less from instinctive tenderness, the same
Fond spirit that blindly works in the blood of all—
Than that a child, more than all other gifts
That earth can offer to declining man,
Brings hope with it, and forward-looking thoughts,
And stirrings of inquietude, when they
By tendency of nature needs must fail.   150
Exceeding was the love he bare to him,
His heart and his heart's joy! For often-times
Old Michael, while he was a babe in arms,
Had done him female service, not alone
For pastime and delight, as is the use
Of fathers, but with patient mind enforced
To acts of tenderness; and he had rocked
His cradle, as with a woman's gentle hand.

And in a later time, ere yet the Boy
Had put on boy's attire, did Michael love,   160
Albeit of a stern unbending mind,
To have the Young-one in his sight, when he
Wrought in the field, or on his shepherd's stool
Sate with a fettered sheep before him stretched
Under the large old oak, that near his door
Stood single, and from matchless depth of shade,
Chosen for the Shearer's covert from the sun,
Thence in our rustic dialect was called

The CLIPPING TREE, a name which yet it bears.
There, while they two were sitting in the shade,   170
With others round them, earnest all and blithe,
Would Michael exercise his heart with looks
Of fond correction and reproof bestowed
Upon the Child, if he disturbed the sheep
By catching at their legs, or with his shouts
Scared them, while they lay still beneath the shears.

And when by Heaven's good grace the boy grew up
A healthy Lad, and carried in his cheek
Two steady roses that were five years old;
Then Michael from a winter coppice cut   180
With his own hand a sapling, which he hooped
With iron, making it throughout in all
Due requisites a perfect shepherd's staff,
And gave it to the Boy; wherewith equipt
He as a watchman oftentimes was placed
At gate or gap, to stem or turn the flock;
And, to his office prematurely called,
There stood the urchin, as you will divine,
Something between a hindrance and a help;
And for this cause not always, I believe,   190
Receiving from his Father hire of praise;
Though nought was left undone which staff, or voice,
Or looks, or threatening gestures, could perform.

But soon as Luke, full ten years old, could stand
Against the mountain blasts; and to the heights,
Not fearing toil, nor length of weary ways,
He with his Father daily went, and they
Were as companions, why should I relate
That objects which the Shepherd loved before
Were dearer now? that from the Boy there came   200
Feelings and emanations—things which were
Light to the sun and music to the wind;
And that the old Man's heart seemed born again?

Thus in his Father's sight the Boy grew up:
And now, when he had reached his eighteenth year,
He was his comfort and his daily hope.
While in this sort the simple household lived
From day to day, to Michael's ear there came
Distressful tidings. Long before the time
Of which I speak, the Shepherd had been bound   210
In surety for his brother's son, a man
Of an industrious life, and ample means;
But unforeseen misfortunes suddenly
Had prest upon him; and old Michael now
Was summoned to discharge the forfeiture,
A grievous penalty, but little less
Than half his substance. This unlooked-for claim,
At the first hearing, for a moment took
More hope out of his life than he supposed
That any old man ever could have lost.   220
As soon as he had armed himself with strength
To look his trouble in the face, it seemed
The Shepherd's sole resource to sell at once
A portion of his patrimonial fields.
Such was his first resolve; he thought again,
And his heart failed him. 'Isabel,' said he,
Two evenings after he had heard the news,
'I have been toiling more than seventy years,
And in the open sunshine of God's love
Have we all lived; yet, if these fields of ours   230
Should pass into a stranger's hand, I think
That I could not lie quiet in my grave.
Our lot is a hard lot; the sun himself
Has scarcely been more diligent than I;
And I have lived to be a fool at last
To my own family. An evil man
That was, and made an evil choice, if he
Were false to us; and, if he were not false,
There are ten thousand to whom loss like this

Had been no sorrow. I forgive him;—but   240
'Twere better to be dumb than to talk thus.
When I began, my purpose was to speak
Of remedies and of a cheerful hope.
Our Luke shall leave us, Isabel; the land
Shall not go from us, and it shall be free;
He shall possess it, free as is the wind
That passes over it. We have, thou know'st,
Another kinsman—he will be our friend
In this distress. He is a prosperous man,
Thriving in trade—and Luke to him shall go,   250
And with his kinsman's help and his own thrift
He quickly will repair this loss, and then
He may return to us. If here he stay,
What can be done? Where every one is poor,
What can be gained?'
                   At this the old Man paused,
And Isabel sat silent, for her mind
Was busy, looking back into past times.
There's Richard Bateman, thought she to herself,
He was a parish-boy—at the church-door
They made a gathering for him, shillings, pence,   260
And halfpennies, wherewith the neighbours bought
A basket, which they filled with pedlar's wares;
And, with this basket on his arm, the lad
Went up to London, found a master there,
Who, out of many, chose the trusty boy
To go and overlook his merchandise
Beyond the seas; where he grew wondrous rich,
And left estates and monies to the poor,
And, at his birth-place, built a chapel floored
With marble, which he sent from foreign lands.   270
These thoughts, and many others of like sort,
Passed quickly through the mind of Isabel,
And her face brightened. The old Man was glad,
And thus resumed:—'Well, Isabel! this scheme

These two days has been meat and drink to me.
Far more than we have lost is left us yet.
We have enough—I wish indeed that I
Were younger;—but this hope is a good hope.
Make ready Luke's best garments, of the best
Buy for him more, and let us send him forth   280
To-morrow, or the next day, or to-night:
If he *could* go, the Boy should go to-night.'

Here Michael ceased, and to the fields went forth
With a light heart. The Housewife for five days
Was restless morn and night, and all day long
Wrought on with her best fingers to prepare
Things needful for the journey of her son.
But Isabel was glad when Sunday came
To stop her in her work: for, when she lay
By Michael's side, she through the last two nights   290
Heard him, how he was troubled in his sleep:
And when they rose at morning she could see
That all his hopes were gone. That day at noon
She said to Luke, while they two by themselves
Were sitting at the door, 'Thou must not go:
We have no other Child but thee to lose,
None to remember—do not go away,
For if thou leave thy Father, he will die.'
The Youth made answer with a jocund voice;
And Isabel, when she had told her fears,   300
Recovered heart. That evening her best fare
Did she bring forth, and all together sat
Like happy people round a Christmas fire.

With daylight Isabel resumed her work;
And all the ensuing week the house appeared
As cheerful as a grove in Spring: at length
The expected letter from their kinsman came,
With kind assurances that he would do

His utmost for the welfare of the Boy;
To which, requests were added, that forthwith   310
He might be sent to him. Ten times or more
The letter was read over; Isabel
Went forth to show it to the neighbours round;
Nor was there at that time on English land
A prouder heart than Luke's. When Isabel
Had to her house returned, the old Man said,
'He shall depart to-morrow.' To this word
The Housewife answered, talking much of things
Which, if at such short notice he should go,
Would surely be forgotten. But at length   320
She gave consent, and Michael was at ease.
Near the tumultuous brook of Green-head Ghyll
In that deep valley, Michael had designed
To build a Sheep-fold; and, before he heard
The tidings of his melancholy loss,
For this same purpose he had gathered up
A heap of stones, which by the streamlet's edge
Lay thrown together, ready for the work.
With Luke that evening thitherward he walked:
And soon as they had reached the place he stopped,   330
And thus the old Man spake to him:—'My Son,
To-morrow thou wilt leave me: with full heart
I look upon them, for thou art the same
That wert a promise to me ere thy birth,
And all thy life hast been my daily joy.
I will relate to thee some little part
Of our two histories; 'twill do thee good
When thou art from me, even if I should touch
On things thou canst not know of.—After thou
First cam'st into the world—as oft befalls   340
To new-born infants—thou didst sleep away
Two days, and blessings from thy Father's tongue
Then fell upon thee. Day by day passed on,
And still I loved thee with increasing love.

Never to living ear came sweeter sounds
Than when I heard thee by our own fire-side
First uttering, without words, a natural tune;
While thou, a feeding babe, didst in thy joy
Sing at thy Mother's breast. Month followed month,
And in the open fields my life was passed   350
And on the mountains; else I think that thou
Hadst been brought up upon thy Father's knees.
But we were playmates, Luke: among these hills,
As well thou knowest, in us the old and young
Have played together, nor with me didst thou
Lack any pleasure which a boy can know.'
Luke had a manly heart; but at these words
He sobbed aloud. The old Man grasped his hand,
And said, 'Nay, do not take it so—I see
That these are things of which I need not speak.   360
—Even to the utmost I have been to thee
A kind and a good Father: and herein
I but repay a gift which I myself
Received at others' hands; for, though now old
Beyond the common life of man, I still
Remember them who loved me in my youth.
Both of them sleep together: here they lived,
As all their Forefathers had done; and, when
At length their time was come, they were not loth
To give their bodies to the family mould.   370
I wished that thou shouldst live the life they lived,
But 'tis a long time to look back, my Son,
And see so little gain from three-score years.
These fields were burthened when they came to me;
Till I was forty years of age, not more
Than half of my inheritance was mine.
I toiled and toiled; God blessed me in my work,
And till these three weeks past the land was free.
—It looks as if it never could endure
Another Master. Heaven forgive me, Luke,   380

If I judge ill for thee, but it seems good
That thou shouldst go.'
                At this the old Man paused;
Then, pointing to the stones near which they stood,
Thus, after a short silence, he resumed:
'This was a work for us; and now, my Son,
It is a work for me. But, lay one stone—
Here, lay it for me, Luke, with thine own hands.
Nay, Boy, be of good hope;—we both may live
To see a better day. At eighty-four
I still am strong and hale;—do thou thy part;   390
I will do mine.—I will begin again
With many tasks that were resigned to thee:
Up to the heights, and in among the storms,
Will I without thee go again, and do
All works which I was wont to do alone,
Before I knew thy face. Heaven bless thee, Boy!
Thy heart these two weeks has been beating fast
With many hopes; it should be so—yes—yes—
I knew that thou couldst never have a wish
To leave me, Luke: thou hast been bound to me   400
Only by links of love: when thou art gone,
What will be left to us!—But I forget
My purposes. Lay now the corner-stone,
As I requested; and hereafter, Luke,
When thou art gone away, should evil men
Be thy companions, think of me, my Son,
And of this moment; hither turn thy thoughts,
And God will strengthen thee: amid all fear
And all temptation, Luke, I pray that thou
May'st bear in mind the life thy Fathers lived,   410
Who, being innocent, did for that cause
Bestir them in good deeds. Now, fare thee well—
When thou return'st, thou in this place wilt see
A work which is not here: a covenant
'Twill be between us; but, whatever fate

Befall thee, I shall love thee to the last,
And bear thy memory with me to the grave.'

The Shepherd ended here; and Luke stooped down,
And, as his Father had requested, laid
The first stone of the Sheep-fold. At the sight   420
The old Man's grief broke from him; to his heart
He pressed his Son, he kissèd him and wept;
And to the house together they returned.

—Hushed was that House in peace, or seeming peace,
Ere the night fell:—with morrow's dawn the Boy
Began his journey, and, when he had reached
The public way, he put on a bold face;
And all the neighbours, as he passed their doors,
Came forth with wishes and with farewell prayers,
That followed him till he was out of sight.   430
A good report did from their Kinsman come,
Of Luke and his well-doing: and the Boy
Wrote loving letters, full of wondrous news,
Which, as the Housewife phrased it, were throughout
'The prettiest letters that were ever seen.'
Both parents read them with rejoicing hearts.
So, many months passed on: and once again
The Shepherd went about his daily work
With confident and cheerful thoughts; and now
Sometimes when he could find a leisure hour   440
He to that valley took his way, and there
Wrought at the Sheep-fold. Meantime Luke began
To slacken in his duty; and, at length,
He in the dissolute city gave himself
To evil courses: ignominy and shame
Fell on him, so that he was driven at last
To seek a hiding-place beyond the seas.

There is a comfort in the strength of love;
'Twill make a thing endurable, which else

Would overset the brain, or break the heart: 450
I have conversed with more than one who well
Remember the old Man, and what he was
Years after he had heard this heavy news.
His bodily frame had been from youth to age
Of an unusual strength. Among the rocks
He went, and still looked up to sun and cloud,
And listened to the wind; and, as before,
Performed all kinds of labour for his sheep,
And for the land, his small inheritance.
And to that hollow dell from time to time   460
Did he repair, to build the Fold of which
His flock had need. 'Tis not forgotten yet
The pity which was then in every heart
For the old Man—and 'tis believed by all
That many and many a day he thither went,
And never lifted up a single stone.

There, by the Sheep-fold, sometimes was he seen
Sitting alone, or with his faithful Dog,
Then old, beside him, lying at his feet.
The length of full seven years, from time to time,   470
He at the building of this Sheep-fold wrought,
And left the work unfinished when he died.
Three years, or little more, did Isabel
Survive her Husband: at her death the estate
Was sold, and went into a stranger's hand.
The cottage which was named the EVENING STAR
Is gone—the ploughshare has been through the ground
On which it stood; great changes have been wrought
In all the neighbourhood:—yet the Oak is left
That grew beside their door; and the remains   480
Of the unfinished Sheep-fold may be seen
Beside the boisterous brook of Green-head Ghyll.

WILLIAM WORDSWORTH

Of William Wordsworth (1770–1850), Matthew Arnold says: 'He is one of the very chief glories of English Poetry: and by nothing is England so glorious as in her poetry.'

Many poets before Wordsworth had described the beauties of nature and expressed their joy in this beauty, but in Wordsworth nature inspired profound and indeed almost mystical experiences, through which he intuited a communion with a 'Universal Spirit'. These communings with nature led, he felt, to a deeper understanding of Man himself, and of Man in relation to God. Many of Wordsworth's poems, like *Michael*, depict simple country people, people of a natural dignity and nobility, and dignified in their suffering. To Wordsworth, the Cumberland 'statesmen', sheep-farmers like Michael, owning their own small farms and sheep-runs, and living hard, simple and almost self-supporting lives, were men of an intrinsic nobility enhanced by their proud independence.

The story itself is a simple and unexciting one. It is Wordsworth's attitude towards it, the profound and dignified pity, and the noble and austere style which make this poem great. Perhaps the climax is reached in the utterly simple, bleak and solemn line—

'And never lifted up a single stone.'

For the sheep-fold was a symbol of all that Michael had held precious. After this, the poem moves quietly to its close.

MORTE D'ARTHUR

So all day long the noise of battle roll'd
Among the mountains by the winter sea;
Until King Arthur's table, man by man,
Had fallen in Lyonnesse about their Lord,
King Arthur: then, because his wound was deep,
The bold Sir Bedivere uplifted him,
Sir Bedivere, the last of all his knights,
And bore him to a chapel nigh the field,
A broken chancel with a broken cross,
That stood on a dark strait of barren land.   10
On one side lay the Ocean, and on one
Lay a great water, and the moon was full.

   Then spake King Arthur to Sir Bedivere:
'The sequel of to-day unsolders all
The goodliest fellowship of famous knights
Whereof this world holds record. Such a sleep
They sleep—the men I loved. I think that we
Shall never more, at any future time,
Delight our souls with talk of knightly deeds,
Walking about the gardens and the halls   20
Of Camelot, as in the days that were.
I perish by this people which I made,—
Tho' Merlin sware that I should come again
To rule once more—but let what will be, be,
I am so deeply smitten thro' the helm
That without help I cannot last till morn.
Thou therefore take my brand Excalibur,
Which was my pride: for thou rememberest how
In those old days, one summer noon, an arm

21 *Camelot*—the place where King Arthur held his court. Malory states Camelot to
be Winchester, but it has also been claimed for Somerset, and for Caerleon in Mon-
mouthshire.

Rose up from out the bosom of the lake,   30
Clothed in white samite, mystic, wonderful,
Holding the sword—and how I row'd across
And took it, and have worn it, like a king:
And, wheresoever I am sung or told
In aftertime, this also shall be known:
But now delay not: take Excalibur,
And fling him far into the middle mere:
Watch what thou seëst, and lightly bring me word.'
  To him replied the bold Sir Bedivere:
'It is not meet, Sir King, to leave thee thus,   40
Aidless, alone, and smitten thro' the helm.
A little thing may harm a wounded man.
Yet I thy hest will all perform at full,
Watch what I see, and lightly bring thee word.'
  So saying, from the ruin'd shrine he stept
And in the moon athwart the place of tombs,
Where lay the mighty bones of ancient men,
Old knights, and over them the sea-wind sang
Shrill, chill, with flakes of foam. He, stepping down
By zig-zag paths, and juts of pointed rock,   50
Came on the shining levels of the lake.
  There drew he forth the brand Excalibur,
And o'er him, drawing it, the winter moon,
Brightening the skirts of a long cloud, ran forth
And sparkled keen with frost against the hilt:
For all the haft twinkled with diamond sparks
Myriads of topaz-lights and jacinth-work
Of subtlest jewellery. He gazed so long
That both his eyes were dazzled as he stood,
This way and that dividing the swift mind,   60
In act to throw: but at the last it seem'd
Better to leave Excalibur concealed

31 *samite*—a rich medieval dress-fabric of silk.
57 *topaz*—a semi-precious stone, yellow, white, green or blue in colour.
57 *jacinth*—a semi-precious stone, orange-red in colour.

There in the many-knotted waterflags
That whistled stiff and dry about the marge.
So strode he back slow to the wounded King.
   Then spake King Arthur to Sir Bedivere:
'Hast thou perform'd my mission which I gave?
What is it thou hast seen? or what hast heard?'
   And answer made the bold Sir Bedivere:
'I heard the ripple washing in the reeds,   70
And the wild water lapping on the crag.'
   To whom replied King Arthur, faint and pale:
'Thou hast betray'd thy nature and thy name,
Not rendering true answer, as beseem'd
Thy fëalty, nor like a noble knight:
For surer sign had follow'd, either hand,
Or voice, or else a motion of the mere.
This is a shameful thing for men to lie.
Yet now, I charge thee, quickly go again
As thou art lief and dear, and do the thing   80
I bad thee, watch, and lightly bring me word.'
   Then went Sir Bedivere the second time
Across the ridge, and paced beside the mere,
Counting the dewy pebbles, fix'd in thought;
But when he saw the wonder of the hilt,
How curiously and strangely chased, he smote
His palms together, and he cried aloud,
   'And if indeed I cast the brand away,
Surely a precious thing, one worthy note,
Should thus be lost for ever from the earth,   90
Which might have pleased the eyes of many men.
What good should follow this, if this were done?
What harm, undone? deep harm to disobey,
Seeing obedience is the bond of rule.
Were it well to obey then, if a king demand
An act unprofitable, against himself?
The King is sick, and knows not what he does.
What record, or what relic of my lord

Should be to aftertime, but empty breath
And rumours of a doubt? but were this kept,   100
Stored in some treasure-house of mighty kings,
Some one might show it at a joust of arms,
Saying, "King Arthur's sword, Excalibur,
Wrought by the lonely maiden of the Lake.
Nine years she wrought it, sitting in the deeps
Upon the hidden bases of the hills."
So might some old man speak in the aftertime
To all the people, winning reverence.
But now much honour and much fame were lost.'

   So spake he, clouded with his own conceit,   110
And hid Excalibur the second time,
And so strode back slow to the wounded King.
   Then spoke King Arthur, breathing heavily:
'What is it thou hast seen? or what hast heard?'
   And answer made the bold Sir Bedivere:
'I heard the water lapping on the crag,
And the long ripple washing in the reeds.'
   To whom replied King Arthur, much in wrath:
'Ah, miserable and unkind, untrue,
Unknightly, traitor-hearted! Woe is me!   120
Authority forgets a dying king,
Laid widow'd of the power in his eye
That bow'd the will. I see thee what thou art;
For thou, the latest-left of all my knights,
In whom should meet the offices of all,
Thou wouldst betray me for the precious hilt;
Either from lust of gold, or like a girl
Valuing the giddy pleasure of the eyes.
Yet, for a man may fail in duty twice,
And the third time may prosper, get thee hence: 130
But, if thou spare to fling Excalibur,
I will arise and slay thee with my hands.'
   Then quickly rose Sir Bedivere, and ran,
And, leaping down the ridges lightly, plunged

Among the bulrush-beds, and clutch'd the sword,
And strongly wheel'd and threw it. The great brand
Made lightnings in the splendour of the moon,
And flashing round and round, and whirl'd in an arch,
Shot like a streamer of the northern morn,
Seen where the moving isles of winter shock   140
By night, with noises of the northern sea.
So flash'd and fell the brand Excalibur:
But ere he dipt the surface, rose an arm
Clothed in white samite, mystic, wonderful,
And caught him by the hilt, and brandish'd him
Three times, and drew him under in the mere.
And lightly went the other to the King.

    Then spoke King Arthur, drawing thicker breath:
'Now see I by thine eyes that this is done.
Speak out: what is it thou hast heard, or seen?'   150

    And answer made the bold Sir Bedivere:
'Sir King, I closed mine eyelids, lest the gems
Should blind my purpose, for I never saw,
Nor shall see, here or elsewhere, till I die,
Not tho' I live three lives of mortal men,
So great a miracle as yonder hilt.
Then with both hands I flung him, wheeling him;
But when I look'd again, behold an arm,
Clothed in white samite, mystic, wonderful,
That caught him by the hilt and brandish'd him   160
Three times, and drew him under in the mere.'

    And answer made King Arthur, breathing hard;
'My end draws nigh; 'tis time that I were gone.
Make broad thy shoulders to receive my weight,
And bear me to the margin; yet I fear
My wound hath taken cold, and I shall die.'

    So saying, from the pavement he half rose,
Slowly, with pain, reclining on his arm,
And looking wistfully with wide blue eyes
As in a picture. Him Sir Bedivere   170

Remorsefully regarded thro' his tears,
And would have spoken, but he found not words,
Then took with care, and kneeling on one knee,
O'er both his shoulders drew the languid hands,
And rising bore him thro' the place of tombs.

But, as he walk'd, King Arthur panted hard,
Like one that feels a nightmare on his bed
When all the house is mute. So sigh'd the King,
Muttering and murmuring at his ear, 'Quick, quick!
I fear it is too late, and I shall die.'   180
But the other swiftly strode from ridge to ridge,
Clothed with his breath, and looking, as he walk'd,
Larger than human on the frozen hills.
He heard the deep behind him, and a cry
Before. His own thought drove him like a goad.
Dry clash'd his harness in the icy caves
And barren chasms, and all to left and right
The bare black cliff clang'd round him, as he based
His feet on juts of slippery crag that rang
Sharp-smitten with the dint of armed heels—   190
And on a sudden, lo! the level lake
And the long glories of the winter moon.

Then saw they how there hove a dusky barge,
Dark as a funeral scarf from stem to stern,
Beneath them; and descending they were ware
That all the decks were dense with stately forms
Black-stoled, black-hooded, like a dream—by these
Three Queens with crowns of gold—and from them rose
A cry that shiver'd to the tingling stars,
And, as it were one voice, an agony   200
Of lamentation, like a wind, that shrills
All night in a waste land, where no one comes,
Or hath come, since the making of the world.

Then murmur'd Arthur, 'Place me in the barge,'
And to the barge they came. There those three Queens
Put forth their hands, and took the King, and wept.

But she, that rose the tallest of them all
And fairest, laid his head upon her lap,
And loosed the shatter'd casque, and chafed his hands,
And call'd him by his name, complaining loud,   210
And dropping bitter tears against his brow
Striped with dark blood: for all his face was white
And colourless, and like the wither'd moon
Smote by the fresh beam of the springing east;
And all his greaves and cuisses dash'd with drops
Of onset; and the light and lustrous curls—
That made his forehead like a rising sun
High from the daïs-throne—were parch'd with dust;
Or, clotted into points and hanging loose,
Mix'd with the knightly growth that fringed his lips.   220
So like a shatter'd column lay the King;
Not like that Arthur who, with lance in rest,
From spur to plume a star of tournament,
Shot thro' the lists at Camelot, and charged
Before the eyes of ladies and of kings.

    Then loudly cried the bold Sir Bedivere,
'Ah! my Lord Arthur, whither shall I go?
Where shall I hide my forehead and my eyes?
For now I see the true old times are dead,
When every morning brought a noble chance,   230
And every chance brought out a noble knight.
Such times have been not since the light that led
The holy Elders with the gift of myrrh.
But now the whole ROUND TABLE is dissolved
Which was an image of the mighty world;
And I, the last, go forth, companionless,
And the days darken round me, and the years,
Among new men, strange faces, other minds.'
    And slowly answered Arthur from the barge:
'The old order changeth, yielding place to new,   240

233 *The holy Elders*—the three wise men, or *Magi*, who came from the East with gifts
of gold, frankincense and myrrh to the infant Christ at Bethlehem. See Eliot's poem,
Journey of the Magi.

And God fulfils Himself in many ways,
Lest one good custom should corrupt the world.
Comfort thyself: what comfort is in me?
I have lived my life, and that which I have done
May He within Himself make pure! but thou,
If thou shouldst never see my face again,
Pray for my soul. More things are wrought by prayer
Than this world dreams of. Wherefore, let thy voice
Rise like a fountain for me night and day.
For what are men better than sheep or goats   250
That nourish a blind life within the brain,
If, knowing God, they lift not hands of prayer
Both for themselves and those who call them friend?
For so the whole round earth is every way
Bound by gold chains about the feet of God.
But now farewell. I am going a long way
With these thou seëst—if indeed I go—
(For all my mind is clouded with a doubt)
To the island-valley of Avilion;
Where falls not hail, or rain, or any snow,   260
Nor ever wind blows loudly; but it lies
Deap-meadow'd, happy, fair with orchard lawns
And bowery hollows crown'd with summer sea,
Where I will heal me of my grievous wound.'
　　So said he, and the barge with oar and sail
Moved from the brink, like some full-breasted swan
That, fluting a wild carol ere her death,
Ruffles her pure cold plume, and takes the flood
With swarthy webs. Long stood Sir Bedivere
Revolving many memories, till the hull   270
Look'd one black dot against the verge of dawn,
And on the mere the wailing died away.

LORD TENNYSON

259 *Avilion*—or, sometimes *Avalon*, is, in Arthurian legend and Celtic mythology, a kind of Earthly Paradise to which the souls of the blessed go after death. A more precise location is claimed for it in the isle of Avalon, near Glastonbury in Somerset.

Alfred, Lord Tennyson (1809–1892) was the most highly esteemed and popular poet of the Victorian era. He won his reputation through the musical and pictorial qualities of his poetry, his idealism, his pride in his country, and above all, because of the expression in his poetry of the doubts and anxieties of the era, particularly in religion, which seemed to be assailed by the findings of science. His 'philosophy' offered a vague but genuine comfort to many troubled minds. To-day we can more readily distinguish between the ephemeral and more permanent elements in his poetry than could people of the early part of the twentieth century, when there was strong reaction against anything Victorian. His finest poetry is magnificently constructed and nobly *felt*. There are beautiful and sensitive pictorial and musical qualities in his best lyrical and narrative poetry.

The subject of this poem was suggested by a passage in *Le Morte D'Arthur*, published in 1485 by Caxton, a compilation and translation of old French Arthurian romances. The simplicity of Malory and the ornateness of Tennyson afford an interesting contrast. The story was acceptable as truth in the Middle Ages, and the bare narration of the 'facts' was wonderful enough. To us and to Tennyson's readers the story is legend and not history, but Tennyson makes it *imaginatively* true. He promotes what Coleridge called 'the willing suspension of disbelief for the moment, which constitutes poetic faith' through the brilliant imagery, the word-music and the subtle changes of rhythm. Notice particularly how he brings out the mystery and beauty of Excalibur, the temptation of Bedivere, the pathos and majesty of Arthur. The relevant passage from Malory's *Morte D'Arthur* is appended, as it affords such an interesting comparison with the treatment by Tennyson of the same episode.

MORTE D'ARTHUR

And Sir Lucan de butlere and Sir Bedivere oft-times heaved him up, and so weakly they led him betwixt them both to a little chapel not far from the sea side. . . . But I may not stand, my head works so. . . . My time hieth fast, said the king. Therefore, said Arthur, take thou Excalibur, my good sword, and go with it to yonder water side, and when thou comest there, I charge thee throw my sword in that water, and come again, and tell me what thou there seest. My lord, said Bedivere, your commandment shall be done, and lightly bring you word again. So Sir Bedivere departed, and by the way he beheld the pommel of that noble sword, that the pommel and haft were all of precious stones, and then he said to himself, If I throw this rich sword in the water, thereof shall never come good but harm and loss. And then Sir Bedivere hid Excalibur under a tree. And as soon as he might he came again unto the king, and said he had been at the water, and had thrown the sword into the water. What sawest thou there? said the king. Sir, he said, I saw nothing but waves and winds. That is untruly said of thee, said the king; therefore go thou lightly again, and do my command as thou art to me lief and dear.

spare not, but throw it in. Then Sir Bedivere returned again, and took the sword in his hand; and then him thought sin and shame to throw away that noble sword; and so eft he hid the sword, and returned again and told to the king that he had been at the water, and done his commandment. What saw thou there? said the king. Sir, he said, I saw nothing but the waters wap and the waves wan. Ah traitor, untrue, said king Arthur, now hast thou betrayed me twice. Who would have wend that thou that hast been to me so lief and dear, and thou art named a noble knight, and would betray me for the riches of the sword. But now go again lightly, for thy long tarrying putteth me in great jeopardy of my life, for I have taken cold. And but if thou do now as I bid thee, if ever I may see thee, I shall slay thee with mine own hands, for thou wouldest for my rich sword see me dead. Then Sir Bedivere departed, and went to the sword, and lightly took it up, and went to the water side, and there he bound the girdle about the hilts, and then he threw the sword as far into the water as he might, and there came an arm and an hand above the water, and met it, and caught it, and so shook it thrice and brandished it, and then vanished away the hand with the sword in the water. So Sir Bedivere came again to the king, and told him what he saw. Alas, said the king, help me hence, for I dread me I have tarried over long. Then Sir Bedivere took the king upon his back, and so went with him to that water side. And when they were at the water side, even fast by the bank hoved a little barge, with many fair ladies in it, and among them all was a queen, and all they had black hoods, and all they wept and shrieked when they saw King Arthur. Now put me into the barge, said the king: and so he did softly. And there received him three queens with great mourning, and so they set him down, and in one of their laps king Arthur laid his head, and then that queen said, Ah, dear brother, why have ye tarried so long from me? Alas, this wound on your head hath caught over much cold. And so then they rowed from the land; and Sir Bedivere beheld all those ladies go from him. Then Sir Bedivere cried, Ah, my lord Arthur, what shall become of me now ye go from me, and leave me here alone among mine enemies. Comfort thyself, said the king, and do as well as thou mayest, for in me is no trust for to trust in. For I will into the vale of Avilion, to heal me of my grievous wound. And if thou hear never more of me, pray for my soul. But ever the queens and the ladies wept and shrieked, that it was pity to hear. And as soon as Sir Bedivere had lost sight of the barge, he wept and wailed, and so took the forest, and so he went all that night and in the morning he was ware betwixt two holts hoar of a chapel and an hermitage.

Le Morte D'Arthur, the Text of Caxton, Globe Edition.

SOHRAB AND RUSTUM

An Episode

And the first grey of morning fill'd the east,
And the fog rose out of the Oxus stream.
But all the Tartar camp along the stream
Was hush'd, and still the men were plunged in sleep;
Sohrab alone, he slept not; all night long
He had lain wakeful, tossing on his bed;
But when the grey dawn stole into his tent,
He rose, and clad himself, and girt his sword,
And took his horsemen's cloak, and left his tent.
And went abroad into the cold wet fog,⁣   10
Through the dim camp to Peran-Wisa's tent.

    Through the black Tartar tents he pass'd, which stood
Clustering like beehives on the low flat strand
Of Oxus, where the summer floods o'erflow
When the sun melts the snows in high Pamere;
Through the black tents he pass'd, o'er that low strand,
And to a hillock came, a little back
From the stream's brink—the spot where first a boat,
Crossing the stream in summer, scrapes the land.
The men of former times had crown'd the top⁣   20
With a clay fort; but that was fall'n, and now
The Tartars built there Peran-Wisa's tent,
A dome of laths, and o'er it felts were spread.
And Sohrab came there, and went in, and stood
Upon the thick-piled carpets in the tent,
And found the old man sleeping on his bed
Of rugs and felts, and near him lay his arms.
And Peran-Wisa heard him, though the step

Oxus—The River Oxus (now called Amu Darya) flows from the mountains of
Afghanistan across the Uzbek steppes to the Aral Sea in Khazakh(U.S.S.R.).

Was dull'd; for he slept light, an old man's sleep;
And he rose quickly on one arm, and said:—   30
    'Who art thou ? for it is not yet clear dawn.
Speak! is there news, or any night alarm ?'
    But Sohrab came to the bedside and said:—
'Thou know'st me, Peran-Wisa! it is I.
The sun is not yet risen, and the foe
Sleep; but I sleep not; all night long I lie
Tossing and wakeful, and I come to thee.
For so did King Afrasiab bid me seek
Thy counsel, and to heed thee as thy son,
In Samarcand, before the army march'd;   40
And I will tell thee what my heart desires.
Thou know'st if, since from Ader-baijan first
I came among the Tartars and bore arms,
I have still served Afrasiab well, and shown,
At my boy's years, the courage of a man.
This too thou know'st, that while I still bear on
The conquering Tartar ensigns through the world,
And beat the Persians back on every field,
I seek one man, one man, and one alone—
Rustum, my father; who I hop'd should greet,   50
Should one day greet, upon some well-fought field,
His not unworthy, not inglorious son.
So I long hop'd, but him I never find.
Come then, hear now, and grant me what I ask.
Let the two armies rest to-day; but I
Will challenge forth the bravest Persian lords
To meet me, man to man; if I prevail,
Rustum will surely hear it; if I fall—
Old man, the dead need no one, claim no kin.
Dim is the rumour of a common fight,   60
Where host meets host, and many names are sunk;
But of a single combat fame speaks clear.'
    He spoke; and Peran-Wisa took the hand
Of the young man in his, and sigh'd, and said:—

'O Sohrab, an unquiet heart is thine!
Canst thou not rest among the Tartar chiefs,
And share the battle's common chance with us
Who love thee, but must press for ever first,
In single fight incurring single risk,
To find a father thou hast never seen?   70
That were far best, my son, to stay with us
Unmurmuring; in our tents, while it is war,
And when 'tis truce, then in Afrasiab's towns.
But, if this one desire indeed rules all,
To seek out Rustum—seek him not through fight!
Seek him in peace, and carry to his arms,
O Sohrab, carry an unwounded son!
But far hence seek him, for he is not here.
For now it is not as when I was young,
When Rustum was in front of every fray;   80
But now he keeps apart, and sits at home,
In Seistan, with Zal, his father old.
Whether that his own mighty strength at last
Feels the abhorr'd approaches of old age,
Or in some quarrel with the Persian King.
There go!—Thou wilt not? Yet my heart forebodes
Danger or death awaits thee on this field.
Fain would I know thee safe and well, though lost
To us; fain therefore send thee hence, in peace
To seek thy father, not seek single fights   90
In vain;—but who can keep the lion's cub
From ravening, and who govern Rustum's son?
Go, I will grant thee what thy heart desires.'
    So said he, and dropp'd Sohrab's hand, and left
His bed, and the warm rugs whereon he lay;
And o'er his chilly limbs his woollen coat
He pass'd, and tied his sandals on his feet,
And threw a white cloak round him, and he took
In his right hand a ruler's staff, no sword;
And on his head he set his sheep-skin cap   100

Black, glossy, curl'd, the fleece of Kara-Kul;
And raised the curtain of his tent, and call'd
His herald to his side, and went abroad.
    The sun by this had risen, and clear'd the fog
From the broad Oxus and the glittering sands.
And from their tents the Tartar horsemen fil'd
Into the open plain; so Haman bade—
Haman, who next to Peran-Wisa rul'd
The host, and still was in his lusty prime.
From their black tents, long files of horse, they stream'd;   110
As when some grey November morn the files,
In marching order spread, of long-neck'd cranes
Stream over Casbin and the southern slopes
Of Elburz, from the Aralian estuaries,
Or some frore Caspian reed-bed, southward bound
For the warm Persian sea-board—so they stream'd,
The Tartars of the Oxus, the King's guard,
First, with black sheep-skin caps and with long spears;
Large men, large steeds; who from Bokhara come
And Khiva, and ferment the milk of mares.   120
Next, the more temperate Toorkmuns of the south,
The Tukas, and the lances of Salore,
And those from Attruck and the Caspian sands;
Light men and on light steeds, who only drink
The acrid milk of camels, and their wells.
And then a swarm of wandering horse, who came
From far, and a more doubtful service own'd;
The Tartars of Ferghana, from the banks
Of the Jaxartes, men with scanty beards
And close-set skull-caps; and those wilder hordes   130
Who roam o'er Kipchak and the northern waste,
Kalmuks and unkempt Kuzzaks, tribes who stray
Nearest the Pole, and wandering Kirghizzes,
Who come on shaggy ponies from Pamere;
These all filed out from camp into the plain.
And on the other side the Persians form'd;—

First a light cloud of horse, Tartars they seem'd,
The Ilyats of Khorassan; and behind,
The royal troops of Persia, horse and foot,
Marshall'd battalions bright in burnish'd steel.   140
But Peran-Wisa with his herald came,
Threading the Tartar squadrons to the front,
And with his staff kept back the foremost ranks.
And when Ferood, who led the Persians, saw
That Peran-Wisa kept the Tartars back,
He took his spear, and to the front he came,
And check'd his ranks, and fix'd them where they stood.
And the old Tartar came upon the sand
Betwixt the silent hosts, and spake, and said:—
    'Ferood, and ye, Persians and Tartars, hear!   150
Let there be truce between the hosts to-day.
But choose a champion from the Persian lords
To fight our champion Sohrab, man to man.'
    As, in the country, on a morn in June,
When the dew glistens on the pearled ears,
A shiver runs through the deep corn for joy—
So, when they heard what Peran-Wisa said,
A thrill through all the Tartar squadrons ran
Of pride and hope for Sohrab, whom they lov'd.
    But as a troop of pedlars, from Cabool,   160
Cross underneath the Indian Caucasus,
That vast sky-neighbouring mountain of milk snow;
Winding so high, that, as they mount, they pass
Long flocks of travelling birds dead on the snow,
Chok'd by the air, and scarce can they themselves
Slake their parch'd throats with sugar'd mulberries—
In single file they move, and stop their breath,
For fear they should dislodge the o'erhanging snows—
So the pale Persians held their breath with fear.
And to Ferood his brother chiefs came up   170
To counsel; Gudurz and Zoarrah came,
And Feraburz, who ruled the Persian host

Second, and was the uncle of the King;
These came and counsell'd, and then Gudurz said:—
   'Ferood, shame bids us take their challenge up,
Yet champion have we none to match this youth.
He has the wild stag's foot, the lion's heart.
But Rustum came last night; aloof he sits
And sullen, and has pitch'd his tents apart.
Him will I seek, and carry to his ear   180
The Tartar challenge, and this young man's name.
Haply he will forget his wrath, and fight.
Stand forth the while, and take their challenge up.'
   So spake he; and Ferood stood forth and said:—
'Old man, be it agreed as thou hast said!
Let Sohrab arm, and we will find a man.'
   He spake: and Peran-Wisa turn'd, and strode
Back through the opening squadrons to his tent
But through the anxious Persians Gudurz ran,
And cross'd the camp which lay behind, and reach'd,   190
Out on the sands beyond it, Rustum's tents.
Of scarlet cloth they were, and glittering gay,
Just pitch'd; the high pavilion in the midst
Was Rustum's, and his men lay camp'd around.
And Gudurz enter'd Rustum's tent, and found
Rustum: his morning meal was done, but still
The table stood before him, charg'd with food—
A side of roasted sheep, and cakes of bread,
And dark green melons; and there Rustum sate
Listless, and held a falcon on his wrist,   200
And play'd with it; but Gudurz came and stood
Before him; and he look'd, and saw him stand,
And with a cry sprang up and dropp'd the bird,
And greeted Gudurz with both hands, and said:—
   'Welcome! these eyes could see no better sight.
What news? but sit down first, and eat and drink.'
   But Gudurz stood in the tent-door, and said:—
'Not now! a time will come to eat and drink,

But not to-day; to-day has other needs.
The armies are drawn out, and stand at gaze;   210
For from the Tartars is a challenge brought
To pick a champion from the Persian lords
To fight their champion—and thou know'st his name—
Sohrab men call him, but his birth is hid.
O Rustum, like thy might is this young man's!
He has the wild stag's foot, the lion's heart;
And he is young, and Iran's chiefs are old,
Or else too weak; and all eyes turn to thee.
Come down and help us, Rustum, or we lose.'

    He spoke; but Rustum answer'd with a smile:—   220
'Go to! if Iran's chiefs are old, then I
Am older; if the young are weak, the King
Errs strangely; for the King, for Kai Khosroo,
Himself is young, and honours younger men,
And lets the aged moulder to their graves.
Rustum he loves no more, but loves the young—
The young may rise at Sohrab's vaunts, not I.
For what care I, though all speak Sohrab's fame?
For would that I myself had such a son,
And not that one slight helpless girl I have—   230
A son so fam'd, so brave, to send to war,
And I to tarry with the snow-hair'd Zal,
My father, whom the robber Afghans vex,
And clip his borders short, and drive his herds,
And he has none to guard his weak old age.
There would I go, and hang my armour up,
And with my great name fence that weak old man,
And spend the goodly treasures I have got,
And rest my age, and hear of Sohrab's fame,
And leave to death the hosts of thankless kings,   240
And with these slaughterous hands draw sword no more.'
    He spoke, and smil'd; and Gudurz made reply:—
'What then, O Rustum, will men say to this,
When Sohrab dares our bravest forth, and seeks

Thee most of all, and thou, whom most he seeks,
Hidest thy face? Take heed lest men should say:
Like some old miser, Rustum hoards his fame,
And shuns to peril it with younger men.'
    And greatly mov'd, then Rustum made reply:—
'O Gudurz, wherefore dost thou say such words?   250
Thou knowest better words than this to say.
What is one more, one less, obscure or fam'd,
Valiant or craven, young or old, to me?
Are not they mortal, am not I myself?
But who for men of nought would do great deeds?
Come, thou shalt see how Rustum hoards his fame!
But I will fight unknown, and in plain arms;
Let not men say of Rustum, he was match'd
In single fight with any mortal man.'
    He spoke, and frown'd; and Gudurz turn'd, and ran   260
Back quickly through the camp in fear and joy—
Fear at his wrath, but joy that Rustum came.
But Rustum strode to his tent-door, and call'd
His followers in, and bade them bring his arms,
And clad himself in steel; the arms he chose
Were plain, and on his shield was no device,
Only his helm was rich, inlaid with gold,
And, from the fluted spine atop, a plume
Of horsehair waved, a scarlet horsehair plume.
So arm'd, he issued forth; and Ruksh, his horse,   270
Follow'd him like a faithful hound at heel—
Ruksh, whose renown was nois'd through all the earth,
The horse, whom Rustum on a foray once
Did in Bokhara by the river find
A colt beneath its dam, and drove him home,
And rear'd him; a bright bay, with lofty crest,
Dight with a saddle-cloth of broider'd green
Crusted with gold, and on the ground were work'd
All beasts of chase, all beasts which hunters know.
So follow'd, Rustum left his tents, and cross'd   280

The camp, and to the Persian host appear'd.
And all the Persians knew him, and with shouts
Hail'd; but the Tartars knew not who he was.
And dear as the wet diver to the eyes
Of his pale wife who waits and weeps on shore,
By sandy Bahrein, in the Persian Gulf,
Plunging all day in the blue waves, at night,
Having made up his tale of precious pearls,
Rejoins her in the hut upon the sands—
So dear to the pale Persians Rustum came. 290

And Rustum to the Persian front advanc'd,
And Sohrab arm'd in Haman's tent, and came.
And as afield the reapers cut a swathe
Down through the middle of a rich man's corn,
And on each side are squares of standing corn,
And in the midst a stubble, short and bare—
So on each side were squares of men, with spears
Bristling, and in the midst, the open sand.
And Rustum came upon the sand, and cast
His eyes toward the Tartar tents, and saw 300
Sohrab come forth, and ey'd him as he came.

As some rich woman, on a winter's morn,
Eyes through her silken curtains the poor drudge
Who with numb blacken'd fingers makes her fire—
At cock-crow, on a starlit winter's morn,
When the frost flowers the whiten'd window-panes—
And wonders how she lives, and what the thoughts
Of that poor drudge may be; so Rustum ey'd
The unknown adventurous youth, who from afar
Came seeking Rustum, and defying forth 310
All the most valiant chiefs; long he perus'd
His spirited air, and wonder'd who he was.
For very young he seem'd, tenderly rear'd;
Like some young cypress, tall, and dark, and straight,
Which in a queen's secluded garden throws
Its slight dark shadow on the moonlit turf,

By midnight, to a bubbling fountain's sound—
So slender Sohrab seem'd, so softly rear'd;
And a deep pity enter'd Rustum's soul
As he beheld him coming; and he stood,   320
And beckon'd to him with his hand, and said:—
      'O thou young man, the air of Heaven is soft,
And warm, and pleasant; but the grave is cold!
Heaven's air is better than the cold dead grave.
Behold me! I am vast, and clad in iron,
And tried; and I have stood on many a field
Of blood, and I have fought with many a foe—
Never was that field lost, or that foe sav'd.
O Sohrab, wherefore wilt thou rush on death?
Be govern'd! quit the Tartar host, and come   330
To Iran, and be as my son to me,
And fight beneath my banner till I die!
There are no youths in Iran brave as thou.'
      So he spake, mildly; Sohrab heard his voice,
The mighty voice of Rustum, and he saw
His giant figure planted on the sand,
Sole, like some single tower, which a chief
Hath builded on the waste in former years
Against the robbers; and he saw that head,
Streak'd with its first grey hairs;—hope fill'd his soul,   340
And he ran forward and embrac'd his knees,
And clasp'd his hand within his own, and said:—
      'O, by thy father's head! by thine own soul!
Art thou not Rustum? speak! art thou not he?'
      But Rustum ey'd askance the kneeling youth,
And turn'd away, and spake to his own soul:—
      'Ah me, I muse what this young fox may mean!
False, wily, boastful are these Tartar boys.
For if I now confess this thing he asks,
And hide it not, but say: *Rustum is here*!   350
He will not yield indeed, nor quit our foes,
But he will find some pretext not to fight,

And praise my fame, and proffer courteous gifts,
A belt or sword perhaps, and go his way.'
And on a feast-tide, in Afrasiab's hall,
In Samarcand, he will arise and cry:
'I challeng'd once, when the two armies camp'd
Beside the Oxus, all the Persian lords
To cope with me in single fight; but they
Shrank, only Rustum dar'd; then he and I   360
Chang'd gifts, and went on equal terms away.
So will he speak, perhaps, while men applaud;
Then were the chiefs of Iran sham'd through me.'

  And then he turn'd, and sternly spake aloud:—
'Rise! wherefore dost thou vainly question thus
Of Rustum? I am here, whom thou hast call'd
By challenge forth; make good thy vaunt, or yield!
Is it with Rustum only thou wouldst fight?
Rash boy, men look on Rustum's face and flee!
For well I know, that did great Rustum stand   370
Before thy face this day, and were reveal'd,
There would be then no talk of fighting more.
But being what I am, I tell thee this—
Do thou record it in thine inmost soul:
Either thou shalt renounce thy vaunt and yield,
Or else thy bones shall strew this sand, till winds
Bleach them, or Oxus with his summer-floods,
Oxus in summer wash them all away.'

  He spoke; and Sohrab answer'd, on his feet:—
'Art thou so fierce? Thou wilt not fright me so!   380
I am no girl, to be made pale by words.
Yet this thou hast said well, did Rustum stand
Here on this field, there were no fighting then.
But Rustum is far hence, and we stand here.
Begin! thou art more vast, more dread than I,
And thou art prov'd, I know, and I am young—
But yet success sways with the breath of Heaven.
And though thou thinkest that thou knowest sure

Thy victory, yet thou canst not surely know.
For we are all, like swimmers in the sea,   390
Pois'd on the top of a huge wave of Fate,
Which hangs uncertain to which side to fall.
And whether it will heave us up to land,
Or whether it will roll us out to sea,
Back out to sea, to the deep waves of death,
We know not, and no search will make us know;
Only the event will teach us in its hour.'
    He spoke, and Rustum answer'd not, but hurl'd
His spear; down from the shoulder, down it came,
As on some partridge in the corn a hawk,   400
That long has tower'd in the airy clouds,
Drops like a plummet; Sohrab saw it come,
And sprang aside, quick as a flash; the spear
Hiss'd, and went quivering down into the sand,
Which it sent flying wide;—then Sohrab threw
In turn, and full struck Rustum's shield; sharp rang,
The iron plates rang sharp, but turn'd the spear.
And Rustum seiz'd his club, which none but he
Could wield; an unlopp'd trunk it was, and huge,
Still rough—like those which men in treeless plains   410
To build them boats fish from the flooded rivers,
Hyphasis or Hydaspes, when, high up
By their dark springs, the wind in winter-time
Hath made in Himalayan forests wrack,
And strewn the channels with torn boughs—so huge
The club which Rustum lifted now, and struck
One stroke; but again Sohrab sprang aside,
Lithe as the glancing snake, and the club came
Thundering to earth, and leapt from Rustum's hand.
And Rustum follow'd his own blow, and fell   420
To his knees, and with his fingers clutch'd the sand;
And now might Sohrab have unsheath'd his sword,
And pierc'd the mighty Rustum while he lay
Dizzy, and on his knees, and chok'd with sand;

But he look'd on, and smil'd, nor bar'd his sword,
But courteously drew back, and spoke, and said:—
  'Thou strik'st too hard! that club of thine will float
Upon the summer floods, and not my bones.
But rise, and be not wroth! not wroth am I;
No, when I see thee, wrath forsakes my soul. 430
Thou say'st, thou art not Rustum; be it so!
Who art thou then, that canst so touch my soul?
Boy as I am, I have seen battles too—
Have waded foremost in their bloody waves
And heard their hollow roar of dying men;
But never was my heart thus touch'd before.
Are they from Heaven, these softenings of the heart?
O thou old warrior, let us yield to Heaven!
Come, plant we here in earth our angry spears,
And make a truce, and sit upon this sand, 440
And pledge each other in red wine, like friends,
And thou shalt talk to me of Rustum's deeds.
There are enough foes in the Persian host,
Whom I may meet, and strike, and feel no pang;
Champions enough Afrasiab has, whom thou
Mayst fight; fight *them*, when they confront thy spear!
But oh, let there be peace 'twixt thee and me!'
  He ceas'd, but while he spake, Rustum had risen,
And stood erect, trembling with rage; his club
He left to lie, but had regain'd his spear, 450
Whose fiery point now in his mail'd right-hand
Blaz'd bright and baleful, like that autumn star,
The baleful sign of fevers; dust had soil'd
His stately crest, and dimm'd his glittering arms.
His breast heav'd, his lips foam'd, and twice his voice
Was chok'd with rage; at last these words broke way:—
  'Girl! nimble with thy feet, not with thy hands!
Curl'd minion, dancer, coiner of sweet words!
Fight; let me hear thy hateful voice no more!
Thou art not in Afrasiab's gardens now 460

With Tartar girls, with whom thou art wont to dance;
But on the Oxus-sands, and in the dance
Of battle, and with me, who make no play
Of war; I fight it out, and hand to hand.
Speak not to me of truce, and pledge, and wine!
Remember all thy valour; try thy feints
And cunning! all the pity I had is gone;
Because thou hast sham'd me before both the hosts
With thy light skipping tricks, and thy girl's wiles.'
    He spoke, and Sohrab kindled at his taunts,   470
And he too drew his sword: at once they rush'd
Together, as two eagles on one prey
Come rushing down together from the clouds,
One from the east, one from the west; their shields
Dash'd with a clang together, and a din
Rose, such as that the sinewy woodcutters
Make often in the forest's heart at morn,
Of hewing axes, crashing trees—such blows
Rustum and Sohrab on each other hail'd.
And you would say that sun and stars took part   480
In that unnatural conflict; for a cloud
Grew suddenly in Heaven, and dark'd the sun
Over the fighters' heads; and a wind rose
Under their feet, and moaning swept the plain,
And in a sandy whirlwind wrapp'd the pair.
In gloom they twain were wrapp'd, and they alone;
For both the on-looking hosts on either hand
Stood in broad daylight, and the sky was pure,
And the sun sparkled on the Oxus stream.
But in the gloom they fought, with bloodshot eyes   490
And labouring breath; first Rustum struck the shield
Which Sohrab held stiff out; the steel-spiked spear
Rent the tough plates, but fail'd to reach the skin,
And Rustum pluck'd it back with angry groan.
Then Sohrab with his sword smote Rustum's helm,
Nor clove its steel quite through; but all the crest

He shore away, and that proud horsehair plume,
Never till now defil'd, sank to the dust;
And Rustum bow'd his head; but then the gloom
Grew blacker, thunder rumbled in the air,   500
And lightnings rent the cloud; and Ruksh, the horse,
Who stood at hand, utter'd a dreadful cry:—
No horse's cry was that, most like the roar
Of some pain'd desert lion, who all day
Has trail'd the hunter's javelin in his side,
And comes at night to die upon the sand.
The two hosts heard that cry, and quak'd for fear,
And Oxus curdled as it cross'd his stream.
But Sohrab heard, and quail'd not, but rush'd on,
And struck again; and again Rustum bow'd   510
His head; but this time all the blade, like glass,
Sprang in a thousand shivers on the helm,
And in the hand the hilt remain'd alone.
Then Rustum rais'd his head; his dreadful eyes
Glared, and he shook on high his menacing spear,
And shouted: *Rustum!*—Sohrab heard that shout,
And shrank amaz'd; back he recoil'd one step
And scann'd with blinking eyes the advancing form;
And then he stood bewilder'd; and he dropp'd
His covering shield, and the spear pierc'd his side.   520
He reel'd, and staggering back, sank to the ground;
And then the gloom dispers'd, and the wind fell,
And the bright sun broke forth, and melted all
The cloud; and the two armies saw the pair—
Saw Rustum standing, safe upon his feet,
And Sohrab, wounded, on the bloody sand.
    Then, with a bitter smile, Rustum began:—
'Sohrab, thou thoughtest in thy mind to kill
A Persian lord this day, and strip his corpse,
And bear thy trophies to Afrasiab's tent.   530
Or else that the great Rustum would come down
Himself to fight, and that thy wiles would move

His heart to take a gift, and let thee go.
And then that all the Tartar host would praise
Thy courage or thy craft, and spread thy fame,
To glad thy father in his weak old age.
Fool, thou art slain, and by an unknown man!
Dearer to the red jackals shalt thou be
Than to thy friends, and to thy father old.'
   And, with a fearless mien, Sohrab replied:
'Unknown thou art; yet thy fierce vaunt is vain.   540
Thou dost not slay me, proud and boastful man!
No! Rustum slays me, and this filial heart.
For were I match'd with ten such men as thou.
And were I he who till to-day I was,
They should be lying here, I standing there.
But that beloved name unnerv'd my arm—
That name, and something, I confess, in thee,
Which troubles all my heart, and made my shield
Fall; and thy spear transfix'd an unarm'd foe.   550
And now thou boastest, and insult'st my fate.
But hear thou this, fierce man, tremble to hear:
The mighty Rustum shall avenge my death!
My father, whom I seek through all the world,
He shall avenge my death, and punish thee!'
   As when some hunter in the spring hath found
A breeding eagle sitting on her nest,
Upon the craggy isle of a hill-lake,
And pierc'd her with an arrow as she rose,
And follow'd her to find her where she fell   560
Far off;—anon her mate comes winging back
From hunting, and a great way off descries
His huddling young left sole: at that, he checks
His pinion, and with short uneasy sweeps
Circles above his eyry, with loud screams
Chiding his mate back to her nest; but she
Lies dying, with the arrow in her side,
In some far stony gorge out of his ken,

A heap of fluttering feathers—never more
Shall the lake glass her, flying over it; 570
Never the black and dripping precipices
Echo her stormy scream as she sails by—
As that poor bird flies home, nor knows his loss,
So Rustum knew not his own loss, but stood
Over his dying son, and knew him not.

But, with a cold, incredulous voice, he said:—
'What prate is this of fathers and revenge?
The mighty Rustum never had a son.'

And, with a failing voice, Sohrab replied:—
'Ah yes, he had! and that lost son am I. 580
Surely the news will one day reach his ear,
Reach Rustum, where he sits, and tarries long,
Somewhere, I know not where, but far from here
And pierce him like a stab, and make him leap
To arms, and cry for vengeance upon thee.
Fierce man, bethink thee, for an only son!
What will that grief, what will that vengeance be?
Oh, could I live, till I that grief had seen!
Yet him I pity not so much, but her
My mother, who in Ader-baijan dwells 590
With that old king, her father, who grows grey
With age, and rules over the valiant Koords.
Her most I pity, who no more will see
Sohrab returning from the Tartar camp,
With spoils and honour, when the war is done.
But a dark rumour will be bruited up,
From tribe to tribe, until it reach her ear;
And then will that defenceless woman learn
That Sohrab will rejoice her sight no more,
But that in battle with a nameless foe, 600
By the far-distant Oxus, he is slain.'

He spoke; and as he ceas'd, he wept aloud,
Thinking of her he left, and his own death.
He spoke; but Rustum listen'd, plung'd in thought.

Nor did he yet believe it was his son
Who spoke, although he call'd back names he knew;
For he had had sure tidings that the babe,
Which was in Ader-baijan born to him,
Had been a puny girl, no boy at all—
So that sad mother sent him word, for fear   610
Rustum should seek the boy, to train in arms;
And so he deem'd that either Sohrab took,
By a false boast, the style of Rustum's son;
Or that men gave it him, to swell his fame.
So deem'd he, yet he listen'd, plunged in thought;
And his soul set to grief, as the vast tide
Of the bright rocking Ocean sets to shore
At the full moon; tears gather'd in his eyes;
For he remember'd his own early youth,
And all its bounding rapture; as, at dawn,   620
The shepherd from his mountain-lodge descries
A far, bright city, smitten by the sun,
Through many rolling clouds—so Rustum saw
His youth; saw Sohrab's mother, in her bloom;
And that old king, her father, who lov'd well
His wandering guest, and gave him his fair child
With joy; and all the pleasant life they led,
They three, in that long-distant summer-time—
The castle, and the dewy woods, and hunt
And hound, and morn on those delightful hills   630
In Ader-baijan. And he saw that Youth,
Of age and looks to be his own dear son,
Piteous and lovely, lying on the sand,
Like some rich hyacinth which by the scythe
Of an unskilful gardener has been cut,
Mowing the garden grass-plots near its bed,
And lies, a fragrant tower of purple bloom,
On the mown, dying grass—so Sohrab lay,
Lovely in death, upon the common sand.
And Rustum gaz'd on him with grief, and said:—   640

'O Sohrab, thou indeed art such a son
Whom Rustum, wert thou his, might well have lov'd!
Yet here thou errest, Sohrab, or else men
Have told thee false—thou art not Rustum's son.
For Rustum had no son; one child he had—
But one—a girl; who with her mother now
Plies some light female task, nor dreams of us—
Of us she dreams not, nor of wounds, nor war.'
    But Sohrab answer'd him in wrath; for now
The anguish of the deep-fix'd spear grew fierce,   650
And he desired to draw forth the steel,
And let the blood flow free, and so to die—
But first he would convince his stubborn foe;
And, rising sternly on one arm, he said:—
    'Man, who art thou who dost deny my words?
Truth sits upon the lips of dying men,
And falsehood, while I liv'd, was far from mine.
I tell thee, prick'd upon this arm I bear
That seal which Rustum to my mother gave,
That she might prick it on the babe she bore.'   660
    He spoke; and all the blood left Rustum's cheeks,
And his knees totter'd, and he smote his hand
Against his breast, his heavy mailed hand,
That the hard iron corslet clank'd aloud;
And to his heart he press'd the other hand,
And in a hollow voice he spake, and said:
    'Sohrab, that were a proof which could not lie!
If thou show this, then art thou Rustum's son.'
    Then, with weak hasty fingers, Sohrab loos'd
His belt, and near the shoulder bar'd his arm,   670
And show'd a sign in faint vermilion points
Prick'd; as a cunning workman, in Pekin,
Pricks with vermilion some clear porcelain vase,
An emperor's gift—at early morn he paints,
And all day long, and, when night comes, the lamp
Lights up his studious forehead and thin hands—

So delicately prick'd the sign appear'd
On Sohrab's arm, the sign of Rustum's seal.
It was that griffin, which of old rear'd Zal,
Rustum's great father, whom they left to die,   680
A helpless babe, among the mountain rocks;
Him that kind creature found, and rear'd, and lov'd—
Then Rustum took it for his glorious sign.
And Sohrab bar'd that figure on his arm,
And himself scann'd it long with mournful eyes,
And then he touch'd it with his hand and said:

  'How say'st thou? Is that sign the proper sign
Of Rustum's son, of or some other man's?'

  He spoke; but Rustum gaz'd, and gaz'd, and stood
Speechless; and then he utter'd one sharp cry: 690
O Boy—thy Father!—and his voice chok'd there.
And then a dark cloud pass'd before his eyes,
And his head swam, and he sank down to earth.
But Sohrab crawl'd to where he lay, and cast
His arms about his neck, and kiss'd his lips,
And with fond faltering fingers strok'd his cheeks,
Trying to call him back to life; and life
Came back to Rustum, and he op'd his eyes,
And they stood wide with horror; and he seiz'd
In both his hands the dust which lay around,   700
And threw it on his head, and smirch'd his hair,—
His hair, and face, and beard, and glittering arms:
And strong convulsive groanings shook his breast,
And his sobs chok'd him; and he clutch'd his sword,
To draw it, and for ever let life out.
But Sohrab saw his thought, and held his hands,
And with a soothing voice he spake, and said:—

  'Father, forbear! for I but meet to-day
The doom which at my birth was written down
In Heaven, and thou art Heaven's unconscious hand.   710
Surely my heart cried out that it was thou,
When first I saw thee; and thy heart spoke too,

I know it! but fate trod these promptings down
Under its iron heel; fate, fate engag'd
The strife, and hurl'd me on my father's spear.
But let us speak no more of this! I find
My father; let me feel that I have found!
Come sit, beside me on this sand, and take
My head betwixt thy hands, and kiss my cheeks,
And wash them with thy tears, and say: *My son!*   720
Quick! quick! for number'd are my sands of life,
And swift; for like the lightning to this field
I came, and like the wind I go away—
Sudden, and swift, and like a passing wind.
But it was writ in Heaven that this should be.'
     So said he, and his voice releas'd the heart
Of Rustum, and his tears broke forth; he cast
His arms round his son's neck, and wept aloud,
And kiss'd him. And awe fell on both the hosts,
When they saw Rustum's grief; and Ruksh, the horse,   730
With his head bowing to the ground and mane
Sweeping the dust, came near, and in mute woe
First to the one then to the other mov'd
His head, as if enquiring what their grief
Might mean; and from his dark, compassionate eyes,
The big warm tears roll'd down, and cak'd the sand.
But Rustum chid him with stern voice, and said:
     'Ruksh, now thou grievest; but, O Ruksh, thy feet
Should first have rotted on their nimble joints,
Or ere they brought thy master to this field!'
     But Sohrab look'd upon the horse and said;—   740
'Is this, then, Ruksh? How often, in past days,
My mother told me of thee, thou brave steed,
My terrible father's terrible horse! and said
That I should one day find thy lord and thee.
Come, let me lay my hand upon thy mane!
O Ruksh, thou art more fortunate than I;
For thou hast gone where I shall never go,

And snuff'd the breezes of my father's home.
And thou hast trod the sands of Seistan,   750
And seen the River of Helmund, and the Lake
Of Zirrah; and the aged Zal himself
Has often strok'd thy neck, and given thee food,
Corn in a golden platter soak'd with wine,
And said; *O Ruksh! bear Rustum well!*—but I
Have never known my grandsire's furrow'd face,
Nor seen his lofty house in Seistan,
Nor slak'd my thirst at the clear Helmund stream;
But lodg'd among my father's foes, and seen
Afrasiab's cities only, Samarcand,   760
Bokhara, and lone Khiva in the waste,
And the black Toorkmun tents; and only drunk
The desert rivers, Moorghab and Tejend,
Kohik, and where the Kalmuks feed their sheep,
The northern Sir; and this great Oxus stream,
The yellow Oxus, by whose brink I die.'
    Then, with a heavy groan, Rustum replied:
'Oh, that its waves were flowing over me!
Oh, that I saw its grains of yellow silt
Roll tumbling in the current o'er my head!'   770
    But, with a grave mild voice, Sohrab replied:—
'Desire not that, my father! thou must live.
For some are born to do great deeds, and live,
As some are born to be obscur'd, and die.
Do thou the deeds I die too young to do,
And reap a second glory in thine age;
Thou art my father, and thy gain is mine.
But come! thou seest this great host of men
Which follow me; I pray thee, slay not these!
Let me entreat for them; what have they done?   780
They follow'd me, my hope, my fame, my star.
Let them all cross the Oxus back in peace.
But me thou must bear hence, not send with them
But carry me with thee to Seistan,

And place me on a bed, and mourn for me,
Thou, and the snow-hair'd Zal, and all thy friends.
And thou must lay me in that lovely earth,
And heap a stately mound above my bones,
And plant a far-seen pillar over all.
That so the passing horseman on the waste   790
May see my tomb a great way off, and say:
Sohrab, the mighty Rustum's son, lies there,
Whom his great father did in ignorance kill!
And I be not forgotten in my grave.'
    And, with a mournful voice, Rustum replied:—
'Fear not! as thou hast said, Sohrab, my son,
So shall it be; for I will burn my tents,
And quit the host, and bear thee hence with me,
And carry thee away to Seistan,
And place thee on a bed, and mourn for thee,   800
With the snow-headed Zal, and all my friends.
And I will lay thee in that lovely earth,
And heap a stately mound above thy bones,
And plant a far-seen pillar over all,
And men shall not forget thee in thy grave.
And I will spare thy host; yea, let them go!
Let them all cross the Oxus back in peace!
What should I do with slaying any more?
For would that all whom I have ever slain
Might be once more alive; my bitterest foes,   810
And they who were call'd champions in their time,
And through whose death I won that fame I have—
And I were nothing but a common man,
A poor, mean soldier, and without renown;
So thou mightest live too, my son, my son!
Or rather would that I, even I myself,
Might now be lying on this bloody sand,
Near death, and by an ignorant stroke of thine,
Not thou of mine! and I might die, not thou;
And I, not thou, be borne to Seistan;   820

And Zal might weep above my grave, not thine;
And say: *O son, I weep thee not too sore,*
For willingly, I know, thou met'st thine end!
But now in blood and battles was my youth,
And full of blood and battles is my age,
And I shall never end this life of blood.'
    Then, at the point of death, Sohrab replied:—
'A life of blood, indeed, thou dreadful man!
But thou shalt yet have peace; only not now,
Not yet! but thou shalt have it on that day,   830
When thou shalt sail in a high-masted ship,
Thou and the other peers of Kai Khosroo,
Returning home over the salt blue sea,
From laying thy dear master in his grave.'
    And Rustum gaz'd in Sohrab's face, and said:—
    'Soon be that day, my son, and deep that sea!
Till then, if fate so wills, let me endure.'
    He spoke; and Sohrab smil'd on him, and took
The spear, and drew it from his side, and eas'd
His wound's imperious anguish; but the blood   840
Came welling from the open gash, and life
Flow'd with the stream;—all down his cold white side
The crimson torrent ran, dim now and soil'd,
Like the soil'd tissue of white violets
Left, freshly gather'd, on their native bank,
By romping children, whom their nurses call
From the hot fields at noon; his head droop'd low,
His limbs grew slack; motionless, white, he lay—
White, with eyes clos'd; only when heavy gasps,
Deep, heavy gasps quivering through all his frame,   850
Convuls'd him back to life, he open'd them,
And fix'd them feebly on his father's face;
Till now all strength was ebb'd, and from his limbs
Unwillingly the spirit fled away,
Regretting the warm mansion which it left,
And youth and bloom, and this delightful world.

So, on the bloody sand, Sohrab lay dead;
And the great Rustum drew his horseman's cloak
Down o'er his face, and sate by his dead son.
As those black granite pillars, once high-rear'd   860
By Jemshid in Persepolis, to bear
His house, now 'mid their broken flights of steps
Lie prone, enormous, down the mountain side—
So in the sand lay Rustum by his son.

And night came down over the solemn waste,
And the two gazing hosts, and that sole pair,
And darken'd all; and a cold fog, with night
Crept from the Oxus. Soon a hum arose,
As of a great assembly loos'd, and fires
Began to twinkle through the fog; for now   870
Both armies mov'd to camp, and took their meal:
The Persians took it on the open sands
Southward, the Tartars by the river marge;
And Rustum and his son were left alone.

But the majestic river floated on,
Out of the mist and hum of that low land,
Into the frosty starlight, and there mov'd,
Rejoicing, through the hush'd Chorasmian waste,
Under the solitary moon;—he flow'd
Right for the polar star, past Orgunjè,   880
Brimming, and bright, and large; then sands begin
To hem his watery march, and dam his streams,
And split his currents; that for many a league
The shorn and parcell'd Oxus strains along
Through beds of sand and matted rushy isles—
Oxus, forgetting the bright speed he had
In his high mountain-cradle in Pamere,
A foil'd circuitous wanderer—till at last
The long'd-for dash of waves is heard, and wide
His luminous home of waters opens, bright   890
And tranquil, from whose floor the new-bath'd stars
Emerge, and shine upon the Aral Sea.   MATTHEW ARNOLD

Matthew Arnold (1822–1888) was an outstanding educationist, an acute and controversial critic of the society and culture of nineteenth-century England, and a poet whose reputation has steadily grown. *Sohrab and Rustum* has been criticised as artificial and derivative. Even in his own time, the pattern of the blank verse, the artificially simple sentence-construction and the ornate similes of the poem were archaic, and the attempted revival of the epic style, influenced chiefly by Milton, was felt to lead nowhere.

And yet Arnold succeeds in this narration, with its grave beauty and profound pathos. As with the Homeric epics, *Beowulf* and the *Morte D'Arthur*, it is a story of the heroes of a warrior society, but these are the heroes of the Tartar tribes of the vast steppes of Central Asia. The single combat between two great warriors is a common feature of the warrior society. Arnold captures well the convention of the great fighter, with all its nobility and savagery, and, too, the acceptance of the fate, the doom against which no man can struggle long. He builds this up with many subtle touches, as well as by the strange doom-struck atmosphere of the fight itself, and by the grim irony of the death of Sohrab through the revelation by his opponent that he is Rustum, and thus the father he had so long sought. The poem moves gravely and slowly, without surprise or suspense. We realise very soon what is to happen. The tragic irony unfolds itself with an inevitability outside human intervention. Arnold found the story in Sir John Malcolm's *History of Persia,* and his poem was published in 1853.

Professor C. S. Lewis, in his autobiography *Surprised by Joy,* describes vividly the impression the poem made on him when at school:

'Much the most important thing that happened to me at Campbell was that I there read *Sohrab and Rustum.* . . . I loved the poem at first sight and have loved it ever since. As the wet fog, in the first line, rose out of the Oxus stream, so out of the whole poem there rose and wrapped me round an exquisite, silvery coolness, a delightful quality of distance and calm, a grave melancholy. I hardly appreciated then, as I have since learned to do, the central tragedy; what enchanted me was the artist in Pekin with his ivory forehead and pale hands, the cypress in the queen's garden, the backward glance at Rustum's youth, the pedlars from Khabul, the hushed Chorasmian waste. Arnold gave me at once . . . a sense, not indeed of passionless vision, but of a passionate, silent gazing at things a long way off. And here observe how literature actually works. Parrot critics say that *Sohrab* is a poem for classicists, to be enjoyed only by those who recognise the Homeric echoes. But I . . . knew nothing of Homer. For me the relation between Arnold and Homer worked the other way; when I came, years later, to read the *Iliad* I liked it partly because it was for me reminiscent of *Sohrab.* Plainly, it does not matter at what point you first break into the system of European poetry. Only keep your ears open and your mouth shut and everything will lead you to everything else in the end.'

'CHILDE ROLAND TO THE DARK TOWER CAME'

(See Edgar's Song in *Lear*)

1

My first thought was, he lied in every word,
   That hoary cripple, with malicious eye
   Askance to watch the working of his lie
On mine, and mouth scarce able to afford
Suppression of the glee that pursed and scored
   Its edge at one more victim gained thereby.

2

What else should he be set for, with his staff?
   What, save to waylay with his lies, ensnare
   All travellers that might find him posted there,
And ask the road? I guessed what skull-like laugh
Would break, what crutch 'gin write my epitaph
   For pastime in the dusty thoroughfare,

3

If at his counsel I should turn aside
   Into that ominous tract which, all agree,
   Hides the Dark Tower. Yet acquiescingly
I did turn as he pointed; neither pride
Nor hope rekindling at the end descried,
   So much as gladness that some end might be.

Childe—a title of honour, meaning 'a young knight' (cp. the ballad *Child Waters* and Byron's *Childe Harold*).

4

For, what with my whole world-wide wandering,
　　What with my search drawn out thro' years, my hope
　　Dwindled into a ghost not fit to cope
With that obstreperous joy success would bring,—
I hardly tried now to rebuke the spring
　　My heart made, finding failure in its scope.

5

As when a sick man very near to death
　　Seems dead indeed, and feels begin and end
　　The tears, and takes the farewell of each friend,
And hears one bid the other go, draw breath
Freelier outside, ('since all is o'er,' he saith,
　　'And the blow fall'n no grieving can amend')

6

While some discuss if near the other graves
　　Be room enough for this, and when a day
　　Suits best for carrying the corpse away,
With care about the banners, scarves and staves,—
And still the man hears all, and only craves
　　He may not shame such tender love and stay.

7

Thus, I had so long suffered in this quest,
　　Heard failure prophesied so oft, been writ
　　So many times among 'The Band'—to wit,
The knights who to the Dark Tower's search addressed
Their steps—that just to fail as they, seemed best,
　　And all the doubt was now—should I be fit.

8

So, quiet as despair, I turned from him,
  That hateful cripple, out of his highway
  Into the path he pointed. All the day
Had been a dreary one at best, and dim
Was settling to its close, yet shot one grim
  Red leer to see the plain catch its estray.

9

For mark! no sooner was I fairly found
  Pledged to the plain, after a pace or two,
  Than pausing to throw backward a last view
To the safe road, 'twas gone! grey plain all round!
Nothing but plain to the horizon's bound.
  I might go on; nought else remained to do.

10

So on I went. I think I never saw
  Such starved ignoble nature; nothing throve:
  For flowers—as well expect a cedar grove!
But cockle, spurge, according to their law
Might propagate their kind, with none to awe,
  You'd think: a burr had been a treasure-trove.

11

No! penury, inertness, and grimace,
  In some strange sort, were the land's portion. 'See
  Or shut your eyes'—said Nature peevishly—
'It nothing skills: I cannot help my case:
'Tis the Last Judgment's fire must cure this place,
  Calcine its clods and set my prisoners free.'

cockle, spurge—cockle, a weed once very prevalent in cornfields; spurge, a wild plant
of various species, to be found on waste ground, particularly on the margins of wood-
lands.

12

If there pushed any ragged thistle-stalk
  Above its mates, the head was chopped—the bents
  Were jealous else. What made those holes and rents
In the dock's harsh swarth leaves—bruised as to baulk
All hope of greenness? 'tis a brute must walk
  Pashing their life out, with a brute's intents.

13

As for the grass, it grew as scant as hair
  In leprosy—thin dry blades pricked the mud
  Which underneath looked kneaded up with blood.
One stiff blind horse, his every bone a-stare,
Stood stupefied, however he came there—
  Thrust out past service from the devil's stud!

14

Alive? he might be dead for all I know,
  With that red, gaunt and colloped neck-a-strain,
  And shut eyes underneath the rusty mane.
Seldom went such grotesqueness with such woe:
I never saw a brute I hated so—
  He must be wicked to deserve such pain.

15

I shut my eyes and turned them on my heart.
  As a man calls for wine before he fights,
  I asked one draught of earlier, happier sights
Ere fitly I could hope to play my part.
Think first, fight afterwards—the soldier's art:
  One taste of the old times sets all to rights!

16

Not it! I fancied Cuthbert's reddening face
  Beneath its garniture of curly gold,
  Dear fellow, till I almost felt him fold
An arm in mine to fix me to the place,
That way he used. Alas! one night's disgrace!
  Out went my heart's new fire and left it cold.

17

Giles, then, the soul of honour—there he stands
  Frank as ten years ago when knighted first.
  What honest men should dare (he said) he durst.
Good—but the scene shifts—faugh! what hangman's hands
Pin to his breast a parchment? his own bands
  Read it. Poor traitor, spit upon and curst!

18

Better this present than a past like that—
  Back therefore to my darkening path again.
  No sound, no sight as far as eye could strain.
Will the night send a howlet or a bat?
I asked: when something on the dismal flat
  Came to arrest my thoughts and change their train.

19

A sudden little river crossed my path
  As unexpected as a serpent comes.
  No sluggish tide congenial to the glooms—
This, as it frothed by, might have been a bath
For the fiend's glowing hoof—to see the wrath
  Of its black eddy bespate with flakes and spumes.

20

So petty yet so spiteful! all along,
  Low scrubby alders kneeled down over it;
  Drenched willows flung them headlong in a fit
Of mute despair, a suicidal throng:
The river which had done them all the wrong,
  Whate'er that was, rolled by, deterred no whit.

21

Which, while I forded,—good saints, how I feared
  To set my foot upon a dead man's cheek,
  Each step, or feel the spear I thrust to seek
For hollows, tangled in his hair or beard!
—It may have been a water-rat I speared,
  But, ugh! it sounded like a baby's shriek.

22

Glad was I when I reached the other bank.
  Now for a better country. Vain presage!
  Who were the strugglers, what war did they wage
Whose savage trample thus could pad the dank
Soil to a plash? toads in a poisoned tank,
  Or wild cats in a red-hot iron cage—

23

The fight must so have seemed in that fell cirque.
  What kept them there, with all the plain to choose?
  No foot-print leading to that horrid mews,
None out of it: mad brewage set to work
Their brains, no doubt, like galley-slaves the Turk
  Pits for his pastime, Christians against Jews.

24

And more than that—a furlong on—why, there!
    What bad use was that engine for, that wheel,
    Or brake, not wheel—that harrow fit to reel
Men's bodies out like silk? with all the air
Of Tophet's tool, on earth left unaware,
    Or brought to sharpen its rusty teeth of steel.

25

Then came a bit of stubbed ground, once a wood,
    Next a marsh, it would seem, and now mere earth
    Desperate and done with; (so a fool finds mirth,
Makes a thing and then mars it, till his mood
Changes and off he goes!) within a rood
    Bog, clay and rubble, sand and stark black dearth.

26

Now blotches rankling, coloured gay and grim,
    Now patches where some leanness of the soil's
    Broke into moss or substances like boils;
Then came some palsied oak, a cleft in him
Like a distorted mouth that splits its rim
    Gaping at death, and dies while it recoils.

27

And just as far as ever from the end!
    Nought in the distance but the evening, nought
    To point my footstep further! At the thought,
A great black bird, Apollyon's bosom-friend,
Sailed past, nor beat his wide wing dragon-penned
    That brushed my cap—perchance the guide I sought.

Tophet—hell: originally a place near Jerusalem where refuse was burned.
Apollyon—the Devil.

28

For looking up, aware I somehow grew,
　'Spite of the dusk, the plain had given place
　All round to mountains—with such name to grace
Mere ugly heights and heaps now stol'n in view.
How thus they had surprised me,—solve it, you!
　How to get from them was no clearer case.

29

Yet half I seemed to recognise some trick
　Of mischief happened to me, God knows when—
　In a bad dream perhaps. Here ended, then,
Progress this way. When, in the very nick
Of giving up, one time more, came a click
　As when a trap shuts—you're inside the den!

30

Burningly it came on me all at once,
　This was the place! those two hills on the right
　Crouched like two bulls locked horn in horn in fight—
While to the left, a tall scalped mountain . . . Dunce,
Fool, to be dozing at the very nonce,
　After a life spent training for the sight!

31

What in the midst lay but the Tower itself?
　The round squat turret, blind as the fool's heart,
　Built of brown stone, without a counterpart
In the whole world. The tempest's mocking elf
Points to the shipman thus the unseen shelf
　He strikes on, only when the timbers start.

32

Not see? because of night perhaps?—Why, day
  Came back again for that! before it left,
  The dying sunset kindled through a cleft:
The hills, like giants at a hunting, lay—
Chin upon hand, to see the game at bay,—
  'Now stab and end the creature—to the heft!'

33

Not hear? when noise was everywhere? it tolled
  Increasing like a bell. Names in my ears,
  Of all the lost adventurers my peers,—
How such a one was strong, and such was bold,
And such was fortunate, yet each of old
  Lost, lost! one moment knelled the woe of years.

34

There they stood, ranged along the hillsides—met
  To view the last of me, a living frame
  For one more picture! in a sheet of flame
I saw them and I knew them all. And yet
Dauntless the slug-horn to my lips I set
  And blew. *'Childe Roland to the Dark Tower came.'*

ROBERT BROWNING

slug-horn—this is an erroneous etymology for the Gaelic *slogan*, a Highland war-cry.
Chatterton, a poet of the late eighteenth century, wrote: 'Some caught a slughorne and
an onsett wounde', and he may have been the first to think that the word *slogan* meant
horn and that it came from *slug-horn*.

Browning (1812–1889) is generally considered as one of the greatest poets
of the nineteenth century, and was also one of the most prodigious in output.
For a long time his work attracted little attention, partly because of its obscurity,
in striking contrast to that of his wife, Elizabeth Browning. Towards the end
of his life, however, his reputation grew, perhaps too rapidly. To-day we feel
more able to separate the wheat from the chaff, and thus to recognise his true
greatness.

This powerful poem was suggested to Browning by the snatch of ballad
flung out in Shakespeare's *King Lear*, amid a farrago of wild nonsense by

Edgar, who is trying to hide his identity under a cover of madness. A few fragments of the ballad have been traced. Browning weaves his story from these few mysterious words. He plunges straight into it, without preparation or introduction—the last episode of a strange quest by a band of knights for 'the Dark Tower'. Only one knight is left alive to achieve the quest, and we have hints from Roland's soliloquy of the fate of the others. The story is vaguely suggested, perhaps, by the Arthurian quest for the Holy Grail, but 'the Dark Tower' seems to be a symbol of Evil which must be destroyed, although the search is a blind one until the Tower is actually seen. Almost to the end, the spirit of Roland is being dragged down to disbelief and despair, but his 'life spent training for the sight' raises his spirit to the final challenge.

The landscape is hideous, but powerfully and vividly described in the colour and significant imagery of Browning's style. It is artistically necessary that the landscape should have this atmosphere of evil despair, not only because it is the home of 'the Dark Tower' but also because it is the final temptation to which Roland is exposed.

Just as Browning was inspired by the snatch of verse in *King Lear*, so Louis Macneice was inspired by Browning's poem to the writing of one of the most brilliant plays ever written exclusively for broadcasting—*The Dark Tower*.

THE HAYSTACK IN THE FLOODS

Had she come all the way for this,
To part at last without a kiss?
Yea, had she borne the dirt and rain
That her own eyes might see him slain
Beside the haystack in the floods?

Along the dripping leafless woods,
The stirrup touching either shoe,
She rode astride as troopers do;
With kirtle kilted to her knee,
To which the mud splash'd wretchedly;   10
And the wet dripp'd from every tree
Upon her head and heavy hair,
And on her eyelids broad and fair;
The tears and rain ran down her face.
By fits and starts they rode apace,
And very often was his place
Far off from her; he had to ride
Ahead, to see what might betide
When the roads cross'd; and sometimes, when
There rose a murmuring from his men,   20
Had to turn back with promises;
Ah me! she had but little ease;
And often for pure doubt and dread
She sobb'd, made giddy in the head
By the swift riding; while, for cold,
Her slender fingers scarce could hold
The wet reins; yea, and scarcely, too,
She felt the foot within her shoe
Against the stirrup: all for this,
To part at last without a kiss   30
Beside the haystack in the floods.

9 *kirtle*—woman's gown or outer petticoat.

For when they near'd that old soak'd hay,
They saw across the only way
That Judas, Godmar, and the three
Red running lions dismally
Grinn'd from his pennon, under which,
In one straight line along the ditch,
They counted thirty heads.

                     So then,
While Robert turn'd round to his men,
She saw at once the wretched end,
And, stooping down, tried hard to rend   40
Her coif the wrong way from her head,
And hid her eyes; while Robert said:
'Nay, love, 'tis scarcely two to one,
At Poictiers where we made them run
So fast—why, sweet my love, good cheer.
The Gascon frontier is so near,
Nought after this.'

                 But, 'O,' she said,
'My God! My God! I have to tread
The long way back without you; then   50
The court at Paris; those six men;
The gratings of the Chatelet;
The swift Seine on some rainy day
Like this, and people standing by,
And laughing, while my weak hands try
To recollect how strong men swim.
All this, or else a life with him,
For which I should be damned at last,
Would God that this next hour were past!'

He answer'd not, but cried his cry,   60
'St. George for Marny!' cheerily;
And laid his hand upon her rein.

Alas! no man of all his train
Gave back that cheery cry again;
And, while for rage his thumb beat fast
Upon his sword-hilts, some one cast
About his neck a kerchief long,
And bound him.

        Then they went along
To Godmar; who said: 'Now, Jehane,
Your lover's life is on the wane   70
So fast, that, if this very hour
You yield not as my paramour,
He will not see the rain leave off—
Nay, keep your tongue from gibe and scoff,
Sir Robert, or I slay you now.'

She laid her hand upon her brow,
Then gazed upon the palm, as though
She thought her forehead bled, and—'No.'
She said, and turn'd her head away,
As there were nothing else to say,   80
And everything was settled: red
Grew Godmar's face from chin to head:
'Jehane, on yonder hill there stands
My castle, guarding well my lands:
What hinders me from taking you,
And doing that I list to do
To your fair wilful body, while
Your knight lies dead?'

            A wicked smile
Wrinkled her face, her lips grew thin,
A long way out she thrust her chin: 90
'You know that I should strangle you
While you were sleeping; or bite through
Your throat, by God's help—ah!' she said,
'Lord Jesus, pity your poor maid!

For in such wise they hem me in,
I cannot choose but sin and sin,
Whatever happens: yet I think
They could not make me eat or drink,
And so should I just reach my rest.'
'Nay, if you do not my behest,   100
O Jehane, though I love you well,'
Said Godmar, 'would I fail to tell
All that I know.' 'Foul lies,' she said.
'Eh? lies my Jehane? by God's head,
At Paris folks would deem them true!
Do you know, Jehane, they cry for you,
'Jehane the brown! Jehane the brown!
Give us Jehane to burn or drown!'—
Eh—gag me Robert!—sweet my friend,
This were indeed a piteous end   110
For those long fingers, and long feet,
And long neck, and smooth shoulders sweet;
An end that few men would forget
That saw it—So, an hour yet:
Consider, Jehane, which to take
Of life or death!'

                          So, scarce awake,
Dismounting, did she leave that place,
And totter some yards: with her face
Turn'd upward to the sky she lay,
Her head on a wet heap of hay,   120
And fell asleep: and while she slept,
And did not dream, the minutes crept
Round to the twelve again; but she,
Being waked at last, sigh'd quietly,
And strangely child-like came and said:
'I will not.' Straightway Godmar's head,
As though it hung on strong wires, turn'd
Most sharply round, and his face burn'd.

For Robert—both his eyes were dry,
He could not weep, but gloomily 130
He seem'd to watch the rain; yea, too,
His lips were firm; he tried once more
To touch her lips; she reach'd out, sore
And vain desire so tortured them,
The poor grey lips, and now the hem
Of his sleeve brush'd them.

                With a start
Up Godmar rose, thrust them apart;
From Robert's throat he loosed the bands
Of silk and mail; with empty hands
Held out, she stood and gazed, and saw, 140
The long bright blade without a flaw
Glide out from Godmar's sheath, his hand
In Robert's hair; she saw him bend
Back Robert's head; she saw him send
The thin steel down; the blow told well,
Right backward the knight Robert fell,
And moan'd as dogs do, being half dead,
Unwitting, as I deem: so then
Godmar turn'd grinning to his men,
Who ran, some five or six, and beat 150
His head to pieces at their feet.

Then Godmar turn'd again, and said:
'So, Jehane, the first fitte is read!
Take note, my lady, that your way
Lies backward to the Chatelet!'
She shook her head and gazed awhile
At her cold hands with a rueful smile,
As though this thing had made her mad.

This was the parting that they had
Beside the haystack in the floods. 160

                WILLIAM MORRIS

153 *fitte*—section or part of the story.

William Morris (1834–1896) was the most versatile of the great Victorians. He published poems, imaginative tales, translations of Greek, Latin and Norse epic poetry, as well as pamphlets on art and politics and a Utopian romance *News From Nowhere.* He designed and made tapestries, wall-papers, furniture, fabrics and carpets, and established a firm to manufacture and sell them. He also designed, printed and bound books of outstanding beauty. In all these things he exercised a profound influence on English taste.

Morris was inspired in much of his work by the life and art of the late Middle Ages. In such poems as this, we see how he turned away from the more romantic conception of the Middle Ages of earlier writers (e.g. Scott, Coleridge, Keats and, in his own time, Tennyson). The poem narrates, tersely and poignantly, an incident of the Hundred Years War between England and France. It is a story of passions and treacheries, powerful in its understatement as it tells of the betrayal, the terrible choice open to Jehane, the death of Robert and Jehane's own fate. There is no false 'glamour' about the rainy day, the dripping landscape, the cold, wet discomfort of the ride, and Jehane's 'poor grey lips'.

The statement of the poem is brusque and direct, the language blunt and simple, with some slight touches of the archaic.

ETIQUETTE

The *Ballyshannon* foundered off the coast of Cariboo,
And down in fathoms many went the captain and the crew;
Down went the owners—greedy men whom hope of gain allured:
Oh, dry the starting tear, for they were heavily insured.

Besides the captain and the mate, the owners and the crew,
The passengers were also drowned excepting only two;
Young Peter Gray, who tasted teas for Baker, Croop, and Co.,
And Somers, who from Eastern shores imported indigo.

These passengers, by reason of their clinging to a mast,
Upon a desert island were eventually cast.
They hunted for their meals, as Alexander Selkirk used,
But they could not chat together—they had not been introduced.

For Peter Gray, and Somers too, though certainly in trade,
Were properly particular about the friends they made;
And somehow thus they settled it without a word of mouth—
That Gray should take the northern half, while Somers took the south.

On Peter's portion oysters grew—a delicacy rare,
But oysters were a delicacy Peter couldn't bear.
On Somers' side was turtle, on the shingle lying thick
Which Somers couldn't eat, because it always made him sick.

Gray gnashed his teeth with envy as he saw a mighty store
Of turtle unmolested on his fellow-creature's shore:
The oysters at his feet aside impatiently he shoved,
For turtle and his mother were the only things he loved.

And Somers sighed in sorrow as he settled in the south,
For the thought of Peter's oysters brought the water to his mouth.
He longed to lay him down upon the shelly bed, and stuff:
He had often eaten oysters, but had never had enough.

How they wished an introduction to each other they had had
When on board the *Ballyshannon*! And it drove them nearly mad
To think how very friendly with each other they might get,
If it wasn't for the arbitrary rule of etiquette!

One day, when out a-hunting for the *mus ridiculus*,
Gray overheard his fellow-man soliloquising thus:
'I wonder how the playmates of my youth are getting on,
M'Connell, S. B. Walters, Paddy Byles, and Robinson?'

These simple words made Peter as delighted as could be,
Old Chummies at the Charterhouse were Robinson and he!
He walked straight up to Somers, then he turned extremely red,
Hesitated, hummed and hawed a bit, then cleared his throat and said:

'I beg your pardon—pray forgive me if I seem too bold,
But you have breathed a name I knew familiarly of old.
You spoke aloud of Robinson—I happened to be by—
You know him?' 'Yes, extremely well.' 'Allow me—so do I.'

It was enough: they felt they could more sociably get on,
For (ah, the magic of the fact!) they each knew Robinson!
And Mr. Somers' turtle was at Peter's service quite,
And Mr. Somers punished Peter's oyster-beds all night.

They soon became like brothers from community of wrongs;
They wrote each other little odes, and sang each other songs;
They told each other anecdotes disparaging their wives;
On several occasions, too, they saved each other's lives.

They felt quite melancholy when they parted for the night,
And got up in the morning soon as ever it was light;
Each other's pleasant company they so relied upon,
And all because it happened that they both knew Robinson!

They lived for many years on that inhospitable shore,
And day by day they learned to love each other more and more.
At last, to their astonishment, on getting up one day,
They saw a vessel anchored in the offing of the bay!

To Peter an idea occurred. 'Suppose we cross the main?
So good an opportunity may not occur again.'
And Somers thought a minute, then ejaculated, 'Done!
I wonder how my business in the City's getting on?'

'But stay,' said Mr. Peter: 'when in England, as you know,
I earned a living tasting teas for Baker, Croop, and Co.
I may be superseded, my employers think me dead!'
'Then come with me,' said Somers, 'and taste indigo instead!'

But all their plans were scattered in a moment when they found
The vessel was a convict ship from Portland, outward bound!
When a boat came off to fetch them, though they felt it very kind,
To go on board they firmly but respectfully declined.

As both the happy settlers roared with laughter at the joke,
They recognised an unattractive fellow pulling stroke:
'Twas Robinson—a convict, in an unbecoming frock!
Condemned to seven years for misappropriating stock!!!

They laughed no more, for Somers thought he had been rather rash
In knowing one whose friend had misappropriated cash;
And Peter thought a foolish tack he must have gone upon,
In making the acquaintance of a friend of Robinson.

At first they didn't quarrel very openly, I've heard;
They nodded when they met, and now and then exchanged a word:
The word grew rare, and rarer still the nodding of the head,
And when they meet each other now, they cut each other dead.

To allocate the island they agreed by word of mouth,
And Peter takes the north again, and Somers take the south:
And Peter has the oysters, which he loathes with horror grim,
And Somers has the turtle—turtle disagrees with him.

W. S. GILBERT

Sir W. S. Gilbert (1836–1911) is famous as the librettist of the Gilbert and Sullivan light operas. The *Bab Ballads*, from which *Etiquette* is taken, had already established his reputation as one of the most accomplished writers of comic verse in an age which had a number of brilliant writers of comic and nonsense poetry (e.g. Calverley, Thackeray, Lewis Carroll and Edward Lear).

The poem is a delicious satire on the formal manners of the English middle classes, all the more pointed by the mock-seriousness: the reader will, of course, understand and sympathise with Gray and Somers in their predicament, for they are, after all, English gentlemen! The long easy lines, the conversational idiom and the cunning simplicity help to build up the naturalness which enhances the preposterousness of the situation.

THE NIGHT OF TRAFALGAR

In the wild October night-time, when the wind raved round the land,
And the Back-sea met the Front-sea,[1] and our doors were blocked
    with sand,
And we heard the drub of Dead-man's Bay, where bones of thousands
    are,
We knew not what the day had done for us at Trafalgar,
          Had done,
          Had done,
      For us at Trafalgar!

'Pull hard, and make the Nothe, or down we go!' one says, says he.
We pulled; and bedtime brought the storm; but snug at home slept we.
Yet all the while our gallants after fighting through the day,
Were beating up and down the dark, sou'-west of Cadiz Bay.
          The dark,
          The dark,
      Sou'-west of Cadiz Bay!

The victors and the vanquished then the storm it tossed and tore,
As hard they strove, those worn-out men, upon that surly shore;
Dead Nelson and his half-dead crew, his foes from near and far,
Were rolled together on the deep that night at Trafalgar!
          The deep,
          The deep,
      That night at Trafalgar!

THOMAS HARDY

[1] In those days the hind part of the harbour adjoining this scene was so named, and at high tides the waves washed across the isthmus at a point called 'The Narrows'.—A Note by Thomas Hardy.
  The scene mentioned by Hardy is Portland. *The Nothe* is an old fort near Weymouth.

Thomas Hardy (1840–1928) is one of our greatest novelists and lyric poets. This poem comes from *The Dynasts*, an 'epic-drama', as he calls it, of the

Napoleonic Wars. Hardy calls it 'A Song', and its inclusion in a collection of narrative poetry may well be questioned. But songs, particularly English songs, frequently have a basis of narrative, or 'sing a story'. This poem gives a vivid impression of storm and battle. It is sung, in *The Dynasts*, by a boat-man, and described as 'that new ballet that they've lately had prented here, and were hawking about town last market-day'. It is interesting to compare it with the ballad on the death of Nelson (see p. 27), which was actually 'hawked about'.

FLANNAN ISLE

'Though three men dwell on Flannan Isle
To keep the lamp alight,
As we steer'd under the lee, we caught
No glimmer through the night!'

A passing ship at dawn had brought
The news; and quickly we set sail,
To find out what strange thing might ail
The keepers of the deep-sea light.

The winter day broke blue and bright,
With glancing sun and glancing spray,
As o'er the swell our boat made way,
As gallant as a gull in flight.

But, as we near'd the lonely Isle;
And look'd up at the naked height;
And saw the lighthouse towering white,
With blinded lantern, that all night
Had never shot a spark
Of comfort through the dark,
So ghostly in the cold sunlight
It seem'd, that we were struck the while
With wonder all too dread for words.

And, as into the tiny creek
We stole beneath the hanging crag,
We saw three queer, black, ugly birds—
Too big, by far, in my belief,
For cormorant or shag—
Like seamen sitting bolt-upright
Upon a half-tide reef:
But, as we near'd, they plunged from sight,
Without a sound, or spurt of white.
And still too mazed to speak,
We landed; and made fast the boat;
And climb'd the track in single file,
Each wishing he was safe afloat,
On any sea, however far,
So be it far from Flannan Isle:
And still we seem'd to climb and climb,
As though we'd lost all count of time,
And so must climb for evermore.
Yet, all too soon, we reached the door—
The black, sun-blister'd lighthouse-door,
That gaped for us ajar.

As, on the threshold, for a spell,
We paused, we seem'd to breathe the smell
Of limewash and of tar,
Familiar as our daily breath,
As though 'twere some strange scent of death:
And so, yet wondering, side by side,
We stood a moment, still tongue-tied:
And each with black foreboding eyed
The door, ere we should fling it wide,
To leave the sunlight for the gloom:
Till, plucking courage up, at last,
Hard on each other's heels we pass'd
Into the living-room.

Yet, as we crowded through the door,
We only saw a table, spread
For dinner, meat and cheese and bread;
But all untouch'd; and no-one there:
As though, when they sat down to eat,
Ere they could even taste,
Alarm had come; and they in haste
Had risen and left the bread and meat:
For at the table-head a chair
Lay tumbled on the floor.
We listen'd; but we only heard
The feeble chirping of a bird
That starved upon its perch:
And, listening still, without a word,
We set about our hopeless search.

We hunted high, we hunted low,
And soon ransack'd the empty house;
Then o'er the Island, to and fro,
We ranged, to listen and to look
In every cranny, cleft or nook
That might have hid a bird or mouse:
But, though we search'd from shore to shore,
We found no sign in any place:
And soon again stood face to face
Before the gaping door:
And stole into the room once more
As frighten'd children steal.

Aye: though we hunted high and low,
And hunted everywhere,
Of the three men's fate we found no trace
Of any kind in any place,
But a door ajar, and an untouch'd meal,
And an overtoppled chair.

And, as we listen'd in the gloom
Of that forsaken living-room—
A chill clutch on our breath—
We thought how ill-chance came to all
Who kept the Flannan Light:
And how the rock had been the death
Of many a likely lad:
How six had come to sudden end,
And three had gone stark mad:
And one whom we'd all known as friend
Had leapt from the lantern one still night,
And fallen dead by the lighthouse wall:
And long we thought
On the three we sought,
And of what yet might befall.

Like curs a glance had brought to heel,
We listen'd, flinching there:
And look'd, and look'd, on the untouch'd meal
And the overtoppled chair.

We seem'd to stand for an endless while,
Though still no word was said,
Three men alive on Flannan Isle,
Who thought on three men dead.

                                   WILFRID GIBSON

Wilfrid Wilson Gibson (1878–1962) is one of the many lesser poets of the first part of this century who have been grouped together, somewhat uncritically, as 'The Georgians'. Their work fell rapidly out of favour in the 'thirties, but their best work is regaining recognition.

Flannan Isle is all the more sinsister and mysterious because we are not given any explanation. The descriptions themselves are realistic—as 'familiar as our daily breath', but there is a complete absence of the extravagant clues that are so often found in 'thrillers'. The 'queer, black, ugly birds' may have significance, but they may easily be cormorants or shags, of which they are an accurate description except for their size, and that could easily be exaggerated by the fear-haunted relief crew.

THE YARN OF THE *LOCH ACHRAY*

The *Loch Achray* was a clipper tall
With seven-and-twenty hands in all.
Twenty to hand and reef and haul,
A skipper to sail and mates to bawl
'Tally on to the tackle-fall,
Heave now 'n' start her, heave 'n' pawl!'
    Hear the yarn of a sailor,
    An old yarn learned at sea.

Her crew were shipped and they said 'Farewell,
So-long, my Tottie, my lovely gell;
We sail to-day if we fetch to hell,
It's time we tackled the wheel a spell.'
    Hear the yarn of a sailor,
    An old yarn learned at sea.

The dockside loafers talked on the quay
The day that she towed down to sea:
'Lord, what a handsome ship she be!
Cheer her, sonny boys, three times three!'
And the dockside loafers gave her a shout
As the red-funnelled tug-boat towed her out;
They gave her a cheer as the custom is,
And the crew yelled, 'Take our loves to Liz—
Three cheers, bullies, for old Pier Head
'N' the bloody stay-at-homes!' they said.
    Hear the yarn of a sailor,
    An old yarn learned at sea.

---

tackle-fall—ropes connecting the blocks of a tackle.
    pawl—lever with a catch for the teeth of a wheel. *To pawl* is to secure the capstan with
a *pawl*, and thus prevent it from recoiling.

In the grey of the coming on of night
She dropped the tug at the Tuskar Light,
'N' the topsails went to the topmast head
To a chorus that nearly awoke the dead.
She trimmed her yards and slanted South
With her royals set and a bone in her mouth.
  Hear the yarn of a sailor,
  An old yarn learned at sea.

She crossed the Line and all went well,
They ate, they slept, and they struck the bell
And I give you a gospel truth when I state
The crowd didn't find any fault with the Mate,
But one night off the River Plate.
  Hear the yarn of a sailor,
  An old yarn learned at sea.

It freshened up till it blew like thunder
And burrowed her deep, lee-scuppers under.
The old man said, 'I mean to hang on
Till her canvas busts or her sticks are gone'—
Which the blushing looney did, till at last
Overboard went her mizzen-mast.
  Hear the yarn of a sailor,
  An old yarn learned at sea.

Then a fierce squall struck the *Loch Achray*
And bowed her down to her water-way;
Her main-shrouds gave and her forestay,
And a green sea carried her wheel away;
Ere the watch below had time to dress
She was cluttered up in a blushing mess.
  Hear the yarn of a sailor,
  An old yarn learned at sea.

royals—sails above the topgallant sails. The ship was under full sail.
 mizzen-mast—after-most mast of a three-masted ship. The captain refused to take in any sail, and the mast gave way under the strain of the gale.
 main-shrouds, forestay—permanent rigging, supporting the masts.

She couldn't lay-to nor yet pay-off,
And she got swept clean in the bloody trough;
Her masts were gone, and afore you knowed
She filled by the head and down she goed.
Her crew made seven-and-twenty dishes
For the big jack-sharks and the little fishes,
And over their bones the water swishes.
　　　Hear the yarn of a sailor,
　　　An old yarn learned at sea.

The wives and girls they watch in the rain
For a ship as won't come home again.
'I reckon it's them head-winds,' they say,
'She'll be home to-morrow, if not to-day.
I'll just nip home 'n' I'll air the sheets
'N' buy the fixin's 'n' cook the meats
As my man like 'n' as my man eats.'
So home they goes by the windy streets,
Thinking their men are homeward bound
With anchors hungry for English ground,
And the bloody fun of it is, they're drowned!
　　　Hear the yarn of a sailor,
　　　An old yarn learned at sea.

JOHN MASEFIELD

John Masefield (1878–1967), poet, dramatist and novelist, was made Poet-Laureate in 1930. Some of his lyrics (e.g. *Sea Fever*) are well known in schools, and his long realistic narrative poems (e.g. *The Everlasting Mercy* and *Reynard the Fox*) brought him a considerable reputation. *Salt Water Ballads*, from which this poem is taken, is his first, and possibly his finest work. Masefield himself had worked on the old sailing ships, and in poems such as this, he shows an intimate knowledge of the hard and tough life they led.

The *clipper* was the final development, and perhaps even the perfection of sail on big ships, graceful, and capable of very great speeds with full sail and strong following winds. The clipper captains drove their ships and their crews mercilessly, and relying on their skilled seamanship, often took great risks to achieve new records. *The Yarn of the Loch Achray* shows how one captain went too far.

Like *The Rime of the Ancient Mariner*, this is 'the yarn of a sailor, An old yarn learned at sea', but it has nothing of the magic and the supernatural of Coleridge's poem. It tells of a clipper on the Cape Horn run, the most arduous of all: a rough realistic tale told by a man who has faced similar hardships and dangers as a job of work and without sentimentality.

THE BLOWING OF THE HORN

From *The Song of Roland*

Roland gripped his horn with might and main,
Put it to his mouth and blew a great strain.
The hills were high and the sound was very plain,
Thirty leagues thence they heard the strain,
Charles heard it, and all his train.
'Our men are fighting,' said Charlemain.
And the Count Guenes answered him again,
'If another said that, we should think him insane.'

Ahoy.

Roland was broken by pain and outworn,
In great anguish he blew his horn;
Out of his mouth the bright blood did fall,
The temples of his brain were now all torn:
He blew a great noise as he held the horn.
Charles heard it in the pass forlorn,
Naimes heard it, the Franks listened all.
Then the King said, 'I hear Roland's horn,
He would never blow it if he were not overborne.'
Guenes answered, 'You are old and outworn,
Such words are worthy of a child new-born,
There is no battle at all, neither won nor lorn.'

Ahoy.

'Moreover, you know of Roland's great pride,
It is a marvel that God lets him bide.
Without your command and knowing you would chide,
He took Noples, and killed the men inside,
With his sword Durendal he smote them hip and side,
Then with water washed the fields where the blood had dried,
So that his killings might never be spied.
All day long he will horn a hare and ride,
Gabbing before his peers, showing his pride,
No man would dare attack him in all the world wide.
Press on your horse now. Why do you abide ?
France is still far from us over the divide.'

                                      Ahoy.

Count Roland's mouth bled from a vein,
Broken were the temples that held his brain,
He blew his horn with grief and in pain,
The Franks heard it and Charlemain.
The King said, 'That horn blows a long strain.'
Duke Naimes answered, 'Roland is in pain,
There is a battle, by my hope of gain,
He here has betrayed him who did so feign;
Put on your war-gear, cry your war-cry again,
Go and succour your noble train,
You hear clearly how Roland does complain.'

                                        Ahoy.

The Emperor made his trumpets blow clear,
The Franks dismounted to put on their gear.
Hawberks and helmets and swords with gold gear,
Men had shields and many a strong spear,
And banners scarlet, white and blue in the air to rear.

On his war-horse mounted each peer,
And spurred right through the pass among the rocks sheer:
Each man said to his comrade dear,
'If we reach Roland ere he be dead on bier,
We will strike good blows with him and make the pagans fear.'
But they had stayed too long, and they were nowhere near.

Ahoy.

JOHN MASEFIELD

Masefield takes this episode from the *Chanson de Roland*, a French epic poem of the eleventh century. In August 778, the rearguard of Charlemagne's army was ambushed and massacred in the valley of Roncevaux by the Basques. The story developed into one of the legends surrounding Charlemagne and was the subject of the great epic poem, the *Chanson*. The enemy become the pagan Saracens (the Moors of Spain). Ganelon, one of the Emperor's councillors and knights, is in treacherous league with the Saracens. He secures the appointment of Roland, whom he hates, as commander of the rearguard, and arranges the ambush in the narrow mountain valley. Pride prevents Roland from sounding his famous ivory horn until at the point of death. Charlemagne returns, too late to save the French chivalry, but he defeats the Saracens, and Ganelon is tried and executed.

The unyielding fight to the death against overwhelming odds is a common theme in the old epic poetry.

LORD LUNDY

WHO WAS TOO FREELY MOVED TO TEARS, AND THEREBY RUINED HIS POLITICAL CAREER

Lord Lundy from his earliest years
Was far too freely moved to Tears.
For instance, if his Mother said,
'Lundy! It's time to go to Bed!'
He bellowed like a little Turk.
Or if his father, Lord Dunquerque,
Said, 'Hi!' in a Commanding Tone,
'Hi, Lundy! Leave the Cat alone!'
Lord Lundy, letting go its tail,
Would raise so terrible a wail
As moved his Grandpapa the Duke
To utter a severe rebuke:
'When I, Sir! was a little Boy,
An Animal was not a Toy!'

His father's Elder Sister, who
Was married to a Parvenoo,
Confided to Her Husband, 'Drat!
The Miserable, Peevish Brat!
Why don't they drown the Little Beast?'
Suggestions which, to say the least,
Are not what we expect to hear
From Daughters of an English Peer.
His Grandmama, his Mother's Mother,
Who had some dignity or other,
The Garter, or no matter what,
I can't remember all the Lot!

Parvenoo—parvenu (French), a person who has gained a high social position through wealth and not birth: an upstart.

Said, 'Oh! that I were Brisk and Spry
To give him that for which to cry!'
(An empty wish, alas! for she
Was Blind and nearly ninety-three.
The Dear Old Butler thought—but there!
I really neither know nor care
For what the Dear Old Butler thought!
In my opinion Butlers ought
To know their place, and not to play
The Old Retainer night and day.
I'm getting tired and so are you,
Let's cut the Poem into two!

Second Canto

It happened to Lord Lundy then,
As happens to so many men:
Towards the age of twenty-six,
They shoved him into politics;
In which profession he commanded
The income that his rank demanded
In turn as Secretary for
India, the Colonies, and War.
But very soon his friends began
To doubt if he were quite the man:
Thus, if a member rose to say
(As members do from day to day),
'Arising out of that reply . . .'
Lord Lundy would begin to cry.
A Hint at harmless little jobs
Would shake him with convulsive sobs.

While as for Revelations, these
Would simply bring him to his knees,
And leave him whimpering like a child.
It drove his Colleagues raving wild!

They let him sink from Post to Post,
From fifteen hundred at the most
To eight, and barely six—and then
To be Curator of Big Ben! . . .
And finally there came a Threat
To oust him from the Cabinet!

The Duke—his aged grandsire—bore
The shame till he could bear no more.
He rallied his declining powers,
Summoned the youth to Brackley Towers,
And bitterly addressed him thus—
'Sir! you have disappointed us!
We had intended you to be
The next Prime Minister but three:
The stocks were sold; the Press was squared;
The Middle Class was quite prepared.
But as it is! . . . My language fails!
Go out and govern New South Wales!'

The Aged Patriot groaned and died:
And gracious! how Lord Lundy cried!

                                        HILAIRE BELLOC

   Hilaire Belloc (1870–1952) was a poet, essayist, novelist, historian, journalist
and politician. This poem is from *Cautionary Verses*, a collection of mock-
moral fables. They have a delightful air of pseudo-primness and mock severity
about them. This poem contains hints of political satire, but it never becomes
so prominent as to spoil the lightness of the wit. To write in this seemingly
casual style and to sustain the sophisticated simplicity requires a technique in
verse-writing of a very high order.

INCIDENT IN HYDE PARK, 1803

The impulses of April, the rain-gems, the rose-cloud,
The frilling of flowers in the westering love-wind!
And here through the Park come gentlemen riding,
And there through the Park come gentlemen riding,
And behind the glossy horses Newfoundland dogs follow.
Says one dog to the other, 'This park, sir, is mine, sir.'
The reply is not wanting: hoarse clashing and mouthing
Arouses the masters.
Then Colonel Montgomery, of the Life-Guards, dismounts.
'Whose dog is this?' The reply is not wanting,
From Captain Macnamara, Royal Navy: 'My dog.'
'Then call your dog off, or by God he'll go sprawling.'
'If my dog goes sprawling, you must knock me down after.'
'Your name?' 'Macnamara, and yours is——' 'Montgomery.'
'And why, sir, not call your dog off?' 'Sir, I chose
Not to do so, no man has dictated to me yet,
And you, I propose, will not change that.' 'This place,
For adjusting disputes is not proper'—and the Colonel,
Back to the saddle, continues, 'If your dog
Fights my dog, I warn you, I knock your dog down.
For the rest, you are welcome to know where to find me,
Colonel Montgomery; and you will of course
Respond with the due information.' 'Be sure of it.'

Now comes the evening, green-twinkling, clear-echoing,
And out to Chalk-farm the Colonel, the Captain,
Each with his group of believers, have driven.
    Primrose Hill on an April evening
    Even now in a fevered London
    Sings a vesper sweet; but these
    Will try another music. Hark!

These are the pistols; let us test them; quite perfect.
Montgomery, Macnamara, six paces, two faces;
Montgomery, Macnamara—both speaking together
In nitre and lead, the style is incisive,
Montgomery fallen, Macnamara half-falling,
The surgeon exploring the work of the evening—
And the Newfoundland dogs stretched at home in the firelight.

The coroner's inquest; the view of one body;
And then, pale, supported, appears at Old Bailey
James Macnamara, to whom this arraignment:
    You stand charged
    That you
    With force and arms
    Did assault Robert Montgomery,
    With a certain pistol
    Of the value of ten shillings,
    Loaded with powder and a leaden bullet,
    Which the gunpowder, feloniously exploded,
    Drove into the body of Robert Montgomery,
    And gave
    One mortal wound;
    Thus you did kill and slay
    The said Robert Montgomery.

O heavy imputation! O dead that yet speaks!
O evening transparency, burst to red thunder!

Speak, Macnamara. He, tremulous as a wind-flower,
Exactly imparts what had slaughtered the Colonel.
'Insignificant the origin of the fact now before you;
Defending our dogs, we grew warm; that was nature;
That heat of itself had not led to disaster.
From defence to defiance was the leap that destroyed.
At once he would have at my deity, Honour—
"If you are offended you know where to find me."

On one side, I saw the wide mouths of Contempt,
Mouth to mouth working, a thousand vile gun-mouths;
On the other, my Honour; Gentlemen of the Jury,
I am a Captain in the British Navy.'

Then said Lord Hood: 'For Captain Macnamara,
He is a gentleman and so says the Navy.'
Then said Lord Nelson: 'I have known Macnamara
Nine years, a gentleman, beloved in the Navy,
Not to be affronted by any man, true,
Yet as I stand here before God and my country,
Macnamara has never offended, and would not,
Man, woman, child!' Then a spring-tide of admirals,
Almost Neptune in person, proclaim Macnamara
Mild, amiable, cautious, as any in the Navy;
And Mr. Garrow rises, to state that if need be,
To assert the even temper and peace of his client,
He would call half the Captains in the British Navy.

Now we are shut from the duel that Honour
Must fight with the Law; no eye can perceive
The fields wherein hundreds of shadowy combats
Must decide between a ghost and a living idolon—
A ghost with his army of the terrors of bloodshed,
A half-ghost with the grand fleet of names that like sunrise
Have dazzled the race with their march on the ocean.
Twenty minutes. How say you?
                              Not guilty.

Then from his chair with his surgeon the Captain
Walks home to his dog, his friends' acclamations
Supplying some colour to the pale looks he had,
Less pale than Montgomery's; and Honour rides on.
                                        EDMUND BLUNDEN

idolon—a false mental image: here, a false conception of the abstract virtue of Honour.

Edmund Blunden (1896–1974), poet, critic and biographer, is best known to the general reader as the author of one of the finest books of the First World War—*Undertones of War*. His poems are chiefly lyrical and pastoral, delicate in observation and subtle in feeling.

Blunden takes the story of this poem from an incident in the life of Rear Admiral James Macnamara (1768–1826). *The Dictionary of National Biography* tells us that "On 6 April 1803 Macnamara fought a duel with a Colonel Montgomery. The quarrel arose out of an accidental encounter between the two men's dogs in Hyde Park the same morning. Both parties were wounded, Montgomery mortally; and the coroner's inquest bringing in a verdict of manslaughter, Macnamara was arrested, and was tried at the Old Bailey on 22 April. His defence was that the provocation and insult came from Montgomery. He called many naval officers, including Hood, Nelson Hotham, Hyde Parker, and Troubridge, as witnesses to his being 'an honourable, good-humoured, pleasant, lively companion, exactly the reverse of a quarrelsome man'. The jury returned a verdict of 'not guilty'."

Blunden pushes to extreme the wicked absurdity of a rigid convention by which gentlemen sometimes trapped themselves into duels in defence of 'honour'. In *Pickwick Papers* Dickens exaggerates it to a wildly comic farce. Blunden's duel might easily have taken place, but he turns it to comedy by his ironic treatment. He has a witty sense of the pompous formality, but he does not let us forget the grim consequences.

JOURNEY OF THE MAGI

'A cold coming we had of it,
Just the worst time of the year
For a journey, and such a long journey:
The ways deep and the weather sharp,
The very dead of winter.'
And the camels galled, sore-footed, refractory,
Lying down in the melted snow.
There were times we regretted
The summer palaces on slopes, the terraces,
And the silken girls bringing sherbet.
Then the camel men cursing and grumbling
And running away. and wanting their liquor and women,
And the night-fires going out, and the lack of shelters,
And the cities hostile and the towns unfriendly
And the villages dirty and charging high prices:
A hard time we had of it.
At the end we preferred to travel all night,
Sleeping in snatches,
With the voices singing in our ears, saying
That this was all folly.

Then at dawn we came down to a temperate valley,
Wet, below the snow-line, smelling of vegetation;
With a running stream and a water-mill beating the darkness,
And three trees on the low sky,
And an old white horse galloped away in the meadow.
Then we came to a tavern with vine-leaves over the lintel,
Six hands at an open door dicing for pieces of silver,
And feet kicking the empty wine-skins.
But there was no information, and so we continued
And arrived at evening, not a moment too soon
Finding the place; it was (you may say) satisfactory.

All this was a long time ago, I remember,
And I would do it again, but set down
This set down
This: were we led all that way for
Birth or Death? There was a Birth, certainly,
We had evidence and no doubt. I had seen birth and death,
But had thought they were different; this Birth was
Hard and bitter agony for us, like Death, our death.
We returned to our places, these Kingdoms,
But no longer at ease here, in the old dispensation,
With an alien people clutching their gods.
I should be glad of another death.

                                        T. S. ELIOT

Thomas Stearns Eliot (1888–1965), of American birth, lived in England
from 1914 and was naturalised as an Englishman in 1927. The publication of
his poem *The Waste Land* in 1922 and of *Poems 1909–1925* revealed striking
innovations in style and choice of theme, and exercised a profound influence on
modern English poetry. Eliot's last poems, *Four Quartets*, published as four
separate poems in 1940–1942, are thought by many to be some of the finest
poetry of our time.

Eliot has also written five notable plays, *Murder in the Cathedral*, *Family
Reunion*, *The Cocktail Party*, *The Confidential Clerk*, and *The Elder Statesman*. In
these he has made a challenging and original attempt to revive poetic drama.
Eliot is also established as one of our most authoritative critics, not only
of literature but also of contemporary society and culture. His work derives
from a profoundly religious and Christian spirit.

There are many lovely pictures of the Magi kneeling before the infant
Christ, and a famous one in Florence, painted by Gozzoli, which depicts a
gorgeous state-procession. Eliot describes the journey very much as it must
have been, with all its inconveniences and hazards. But the poem is essentially
religious, and we can never come to the end of our thinking as we ponder
over the last lines.

The three trees, the vine-leaves and the dicing are not mere details to fill
in the picture. They hint at the death of the one who has just been born.

The poem takes its source directly from a sermon by Lancelot Andrewes
(1555–1626), Bishop of Winchester, on the text, 'Behold there came wise men
from the East'. Andrewes says:

'This was riding many a hundred miles, and cost them many a day's
journey. . . . This was nothing pleasant, for through deserts, all the way

waste and desolate. Nor easy neither; for over the rocks and crags of both Arabias. . . . Exceeding dangerous, as lying through the midst of the "black tents of Kedar", a nation of thieves and cut-throats; to pass over the hills of robbers, infamous then, and infamous to this day. . . . It was no summer progress. A cold coming they had of it at this time of the year, just the worst time of the year to take a journey, and especially a long journey in. The ways deep, the weather sharp, the days short, the sun farthest off *in solstitio brumali*, "the very dead of winter".'

BALLAD OF THE GOODLY FERE

SIMON ZELOTES SPEAKETH IT SOMEWHILE AFTER THE CRUCIFIXION

Ha' we lost the goodliest fere o' all
For the priests and the gallows tree?
Aye lover he was of brawny men,
O' ships and the open sea.

When they came wi' a host to take Our Man
His smile was good to see,
'First let these go!' quo' our Goodly Fere,
'Or I'll see ye damned,' says he.

Aye he sent us out through the crossed high spears
And the scorn of his laugh rang free,
'Why took ye not me when I walked about
Alone in the town?' says he.

Oh we drunk his 'Hale' in the good red wine
When we last made company,
No capon priest was the Goodly Fere
But a man o' men was he.

fere—mate, companion.
Simon Zelotes—Simon the Zealous: see *Luke* vi. 13-15.

I ha' seen him drive a hundred men
Wi' a bundle o' cords swung free,
That they took the high and holy house
For their pawn and treasury.

They'll no' get him a' in a book I think
Though they write it cunningly;
No mouse of the scrolls was the Goodly Fere
But aye loved the open sea.

If they think they ha' snared our Goodly Fere
They are fools to the last degree.
'I'll go to the feast,' quo' our Goodly Fere,
'Though I go to the gallows tree.'

'Ye ha' seen me heal the lame and blind,
And wake the dead,' says he,
'Ye shall see one thing to master all:
'Tis how a brave man dies on the tree.'

A son of God was the Goodly Fere
That bade us his brothers be.
I ha' seen him cow a thousand men.
I ha' seen him upon the tree.

He cried no cry when they drave the nails
And the blood gushed hot and free,
The hounds of the crimson sky gave tongue
But never a cry cried he.

I ha' seen him cow a thousand men
On the hills o' Galilee,
They whined as he walked out calm between,
Wi' his eyes like the grey o' the sea.

Like the sea that brooks no voyaging
With the winds unleashed and free,
Like the sea that he cowed at Genseret
Wi' twey words spoke' suddenly.

A master of men was the Goodly Fere,
A mate of the wind and sea,
If they think they ha' slain our Goodly Fere
They are fools eternally.

I ha' seen him eat o' the honey-comb
Sin' they nailed him to the tree.

EZRA POUND

Ezra Pound (1885–1972) is an American poet of remarkable and wide scholarship. His greatest work is generally considered to be the series *Seventy Cantos* and *The Pisan Cantos*.

The Ballad of the Goodly Fere, a striking and original poem, could be described as 'allusive narrative'. The poem could have no meaning to those who were ignorant of the life of Christ. The poem is written for those who are acquainted with the story but who have lost something of their awareness of its impact. Pound makes us see it again as one of the apostles might have, very soon after the Crucifixion. It is remarkable how vividly and with what economy Pound includes so many of the events narrated in the New Testament. His poem emphasises the power rather than the gentleness of Christ, but it also reveals the passionate devotion of one of the Apostles to his Master.

THE NABARA

'They preferred, because of the rudeness of their heart,
to die rather than to surrender'

PHASE ONE

Freedom is more than a word, more than the base coinage
Of statesmen, the tyrant's dishonoured cheque, or the dreamer's mad
Inflated currency. She is mortal, we know, and made
In the image of simple men who have no taste for carnage
But sooner kill and are killed than see that image betrayed.
Mortal she is, yet rising always refreshed from her ashes:
She is bound to earth, yet she flies as high as a passage bird
To home wherever man's heart with seasonal warmth is stirred:
Innocent is her touch as the dawn's, but still it unleashes
The ravisher shades of envy. Freedom is more than a word.

I see man's heart two-edged, keen both for death and creation.
As a sculptor rejoices, stabbing and mutilating the stone
Into a shapelier life, and the two joys make one—
So man is wrought in his hour of agony and elation
To efface the flesh to reveal the crying need of his bone.
Burning the issue was beyond their mild forecasting
For those I tell of—men used to the tolerable joy and hurt
Of simple lives: they coveted never an epic part;
But history's hand was upon them and hewed an everlasting
Image of freedom out of their rude and stubborn heart.

The year, Nineteen-thirty-seven: month, March: the men, descendants
Of those Iberian fathers, the inquiring ones who would go
Wherever the sea-ways led: a pacific people, slow
To feel ambition, loving their laws and their independence—
Men of the Basque country, the Mar Cantabrico.

174

Fishermen, with no guile outside their craft, they had weathered
Often the sierra-ranked Biscayan surges, the wet
Fog of the Newfoundland Banks: they were fond of *pelota*: they met
No game beyond their skill as they swept the sea together,
Until the morning they found the leviathan in their net.

Government trawlers *Nabara, Guipuzkoa, Bizkaya,*
Donostia, escorting across blockaded seas
Galdames with her cargo of nickel and refugees
From Bayonne to Bilbao, while the crest of war curled higher
Inland over the glacial valleys, the ancient ease.
On the morning of March the fifth, a chill North-Wester fanned them,
Fogging the glassy waves: what uncharted doom lay low
There in the fog athwart their course, they could not know:
Stout were the armed trawlers, redoubtable those who manned them—
Men of the Basque country, the Mar Cantabrico.

Slowly they nosed ahead, while under the chill North-Wester
Nervous the sea crawled and twitched like the skin of a beast
That dreams of the chase, the kill, the blood-beslavered feast:
They, too, the light-hearted sailors, dreamed of a fine fiesta,
Flags and the children waving, when they won home from the east.
Vague as images seen in a misted glass or the vision
Of crystal-gazer, the ships huddled, receded, neared,
Threading the weird fog-maze that coiled their funnels and bleared
Day's eye. They were glad of the fog till *Galdames* lost position
—Their convoy, precious in life and metal—and disappeared.

But still they held their course, the confident ear-ringed captains,
Unerring towards the landfall, nor guessed how the land lay,
How the guardian fog was a guide to lead them all astray.

---

    sierra-ranked—the great, broken waves of the stormy Bay of Biscay are like the *sierras*,
the long, jagged mountain ranges of Spain.
    pelota—a popular Basque game played with a ball and the palm of the hand or a racket.

For now, at a wink, the mist rolled up like the film that curtains
A saurian's eye; and into the glare of an evil day
Bizkaya, Guipuzkoa, Nabara, and the little
Donostia stepped at intervals; and sighted, alas,
Blocking the sea and sky a mountain they might not pass,
An isle thrown up volcanic and smoking, a giant in metal
Astride their path—the rebel cruiser, *Canarias.*

A ship of ten thousand tons she was, a heavyweight fighter
To the cocky bantam trawlers: and under her armament
Of eight- and four-inch guns there followed obedient
Towards Pasajes a prize just seized, an Estonian freighter
Laden with arms the exporters of death to Spain had sent.
A hush, the first qualm of conflict, falls on the cruiser's burnished
Turrets, the trawlers' grimy decks: fiercer the lime-
Light falls, and out of the solemn ring the late mists climb,
And ship to ship the antagonists gaze at each other astonished
Across the quaking gulf of the sea for a moment's time.

The trawlers' men had no chance or wish to elude the fated
Encounter. Freedom to these was natural pride that runs
Hot as the blood, their climate and heritage, dearer than sons.
Bizkaya, Guipuzkoa, knowing themselves outweighted,
Drew closer to draw first blood with their pairs of four-inch guns.
Aboard *Canarias* the German gun-layers stationed
Brisk at their intricate batteries—guns and men both trained
To a hair in accuracy, aimed at a pitiless end—
Fired, and the smoke rolled forth over the unimpassioned
Face of a day where nothing certain but death remained.

---

saurian—an order of lizards, which includes the crocodile, the alligator and the extinct ichthyosaurus. Lizards (and birds) have, in addition to eyelids, a transparent membrane moved by a special muscular apparatus. It is easily seen as a grey, movable film, over the eyes of fowls and parrots.

PHASE TWO

The sound of the first salvo skimmed the ocean and thumped
Cape Machichaco's granite ribs: it rebounded where
The salt-sprayed trees grow tough from wrestling the wind: it jumped
From isle to rocky isle: it was heard by women while
They walked to shrine or market, a warning they must fear.
But, beyond their alarm, as
Though that sound were also a signal for fate to strip
Luck's last green shoot from the falling stock of the Basques, *Galdames*
Emerged out of the mist that lingered to the west
Under the reeking muzzles of the rebel battleship.

Which instantly threw five shells over her funnel, and threw
Her hundred women and children into a slaughter-yard panic
On the deck they imagined smoking with worse than the foggy dew,
So that *Galdames* rolled as they slipped, clawed, trampled, reeled
Away from the gape of the cruiser's guns. A spasm galvanic,
Fear's chemistry, shocked the women's bodies, a moment before
Huddled like sheep in a mist, inert as bales of rag,
A mere deck-cargo; but more
Than furies now, for they stormed *Galdames*' bridge and swarmed
Over her captain and forced him to run up the white flag.

Signalling the Estonian, 'Heave-to', *Canarias* steamed
Leisurely over to make sure of this other prize:
Over-leisurely was her reckoning—she never dreamed
The Estonian in that pause could be snatched from her shark-shape
   jaws
By ships of minnow size.
Meanwhile *Nabara* and *Guipuzkoa*, not reluctant
For closer grips while their guns and crew were still entire,
Thrust forward: twice *Guipuzkoa* with a deadly jolt was rocked, and
The sea spat up in geysers of boiling foam, as the cruiser's
Heavier guns boxed them in a torrid zone of fire.

And now the little *Donostia* who lay with her 75s
Dumb in the offing—her weapons against that leviathan
Impotent as pen-knives—
Witnessed a bold manœuvre, a move of genius, never
In naval history told. She saw *Biskaya* run
Ahead of her consorts, a berserk atom of steel, audacious,
Her signal-flags soon to flutter like banderillas, straight
Towards the Estonian speeding, a young bull over the spacious
And foam-distraught arena, till the sides of the freight-ship screen her
From *Canarias* that will see the point of her charge too late.

'Who are you and where are you going?' the flags of *Biskaya* ques-
    tioned.
'Carrying arms and forced to go to Pasajes,' replied
The Estonian. 'Follow me to harbour.' 'Cannot, am threatened.'
Biskaya's last word—'Turn at once!'—and she points her peremptory
    guns
Against the freighter's mountainous flanks that blankly hide
This fluttering language and flaunt of signal insolence
From the eyes of *Canarias*. At last the rebels can see
That the two ships' talk meant a practical joke at their expense:
They see the Estonian veering away, to Bermeo steering,
Biskaya under her lee.

(To the Basques that ship was a tonic, for she carried some million
    rounds
Of ammunition: to hearts grown sick with hope deferred
And the drain of their country's wounds
She brought what most they needed in face of the aid evaded
And the cold delay of those to whom freedom was only a word).
Owlish upon the water sat the *Canarias*
Mobbed by those darting trawlers, and her signals blinked in vain
After the freighter, that she still believed too large to pass
Into Bermeo's port—a prize she fondly thought,

----

banderillas—long, light darts with ribbons attached, which are stuck into the neck of
the bull by the *banderilleros*, as a preliminary to the playing and killing of the bull by the
matador.

When she'd blown the trawlers out of the water, she'd take again.
Brisk at their intricate batteries the German gun-layers go
About death's business, knowing their longer reach must foil
The impetus, break the heart of the government ships: each blow
Deliberately they aim, and tiger-striped with flame
Is the jungle mirk of the smoke as their guns leap and recoil.
The Newfoundland trawlers feel
A hail and hurricane the like they have never known
In all their deep-sea life: they wince at the squalls of steel
That burst on their open decks, rake them and leave them wrecks,
But still they fight on long into the sunless afternoon.

—Fought on, four guns against the best of the rebel navy,
Until *Guipuzkoa's* crew could stanch the fires no more
That gushed from her gashes and seeped nearer the magazine. Heavy
At heart they turned away for the Nervion that day:
Their ship, *Guipuzkoa*, wore
Flame's rose on her heart like a decoration of highest honour
As listing she reeled into Las Arenas; and in a row
On her deck there lay, smoke-palled, that oriflamme's crackling
   banner
Above them, her dead—a quarter of the fishermen who had fought
   her—
Men of the Basque country, the Mar Cantabrico.

   oriflamme—the sacred banner of red silk received by early French kings from the abbot
of St. Denis on starting for war: a rallying-point in a struggle.

PHASE THREE

And now the gallant *Nabara* was left in the ring alone,
The sky hollow around her, the fawning sea at her side:
But the ear-ringed crew in their berets stood to the guns and cried
A fresh defiance down
The ebb of the afternoon, the battle's darkening tide.
Honour was satisfied long since; they had held and harried
A ship ten times their size; they well could have called it a day.
But they hoped, if a little longer they kept the cruiser in play,
Galdames with the wealth of life and metal she carried
Might make her getaway.

Canarias, though easily she outpaced and out-gunned her,
Finding this midge could sting
Edged off, and beneath a wedge of smoke steamed in a ring
On the rim of the trawler's range, a circular storm of thunder.
But always *Nabara* turned her broadside, manœuvring
To keep both guns on the target, scorning safety devices.
Slower now battle's tempo, irregular the beat
Of gunfire in the heart
Of the afternoon, the distempered sky sank to the crisis,
Shell-shocked the sea tossed and hissed in delirious heat.

The battle's tempo slowed, for the cruiser could take her time,
And the guns of *Nabara* grew
Red-hot, and of fifty-two Basque seamen had been her crew
Many were dead already, the rest filthy with grime
And their comrades' blood, weary with wounds all but a few.
Between two fires they fought, for the sparks that flashing spoke
From the cruiser's thunder-bulk were answered on their own craft
By traitor flames that crawled out of every cranny and rift
Blinding them all with smoke.
At half-past-four *Nabara* was burning fore and aft.

What buoyancy of will
Was theirs to keep her afloat, no vessel now but a sieve—
So jarred and scarred, the rivets starting, no inch of her safe
From the guns of the foe that wrapped her in a cyclone of shrieking
    steel!
Southward the sheltering havens showed clear, the cliffs and the surf
Familiar to them from childhood, the shapes of a life still dear:
But dearer still to see
Those insured for life from the shadow of tyranny.
Freedom was not on their lips; it was what made them endure,
A steel spring in the yielding flesh, a thirst to be free.

And now from the little *Donostia* that lay with her 75s
Dumb in the offing, they saw *Nabara* painfully lower
A boat, which crawled like a shattered crab slower and slower
Towards them. They cheered the survivors, thankful to save these
    lives
At least. They saw each rower,
As the boat dragged alongside, was wounded—the oars they held
Dripping with blood, a bloody skein reeled out in their wake:
And they swarmed down the rope-ladders to rescue these men so weak
From wounds they must be hauled
Aboard like babies. And then they saw they had made a mistake.

For, standing up in the boat,
A man of that grimy boat's-crew hailed them: 'Our officer asks
You give us your bandages and all your water-casks,
Then run for Bermeo. We're going to finish this game of *pelota*.'
Donostia's captain begged them with tears to escape: but the Basques
Would play their game to the end.
They took the bandages, and cursing at his delay
They took the casks that might keep the fires on their ship at bay;
And they rowed back to *Nabara*, trailing their blood behind
Over the water, the sunset and crimson ebb of their day.

For two hours more they fought, while *Nabara* beneath their feet
Was turned to a heap of smouldering scrap-iron. Once again
The flames they had checked awhile broke out. When the forward gun
Was hit, they turned about
Bringing the after gun to bear. They fought in pain
And the instant knowledge of death: but the waters filling their riven
Ship could not quench the love that fired them. As each man fell
To the deck, his body took fire as if death made visible
That burning spirit. For two more hours they fought, and at seven
They fired their last shell.

Of her officers all but one were dead. Of her engineers
All but one were dead. Of the fifty-two that had sailed
In her, all were dead but fourteen—and each of these half-killed
With wounds. And the night-dew fell in a hush of ashen tears,
And *Nabara's* tongue was stilled.
Southward the sheltering havens grew dark, the cliffs and the green
Shallows they knew; where their friends had watched them as evening
    wore
To a glowing end, who swore
Nabara must show a white flag now, but saw instead the fourteen
Climb into their matchwood boat and fainting pull for the shore.

Canarias lowered a launch that swept in a greyhound's curve
Pitiless to pursue
And cut them off. But that bloodless and all-but-phantom crew
Still gave no soft concessions to fate: they strung their nerve
For one last fling of defiance, they shipped their oars and threw
Hand-grenades at the launch as it circled about to board them.
But the strength of the hands that had carved them a hold on history
Failed them at last: the grenades fell short of the enemy,
Who grappled and overpowered them,
While *Nabara* sank by the stern in the hushed Cantabrian sea.

·   ·   ·   ·   ·   ·

They bore not a charmed life. They went into battle foreseeing
Probable loss, and they lost. The tides of Biscay flow
Over the obstinate bones of many, the winds are sighing
Round prison walls where the rest are doomed like their ship to rust—
Men of the Basque country, the Mar Cantabrico.
Simple men who asked of their life no mythical splendour,
They loved its familiar ways so well that they preferred
In the rudeness of their heart to die rather than to surrender. . . .
Mortal these words and the deed they remember, but cast a seed
Shall flower for an age when freedom is man's creative word.

Freedom was more than a word, more than the base coinage
Of politicians, who hiding behind the skirts of peace
They had defiled, gave up that country to rack and carnage:
For whom, indelibly stamped with history's contempt,
Remains but to haunt the blackened shell of their policies.
For these I have told of, freedom was flesh and blood—a mortal
Body, the gun-breech hot to its touch: yet the battle's height
Raised it to love's meridian and held it awhile immortal;
And its light through time still flashes like a star's that has turned to
    ashes,
Long after *Nabara's* passion was quenched in the sea's heart.

C. DAY LEWIS

C. Day Lewis (1904–1972) came to the fore in the early 'thirties as one of the younger poets who wrote of contemporary themes in a contemporary idiom and imagery. He held the Professorship of Poetry at Oxford, 1951–6. He was a distinguished literary critic, a translator of Vergil into English verse, a writer of novels for young people, and. under the name of Nicholas Blake, a writer of detective stories.

This sea-fight occurred off the north coast of Spain, near Bilbao, during the Spanish Civil War (1935–1938), between Government trawlers and an insurgent cruiser. The democratic countries had placed an embargo on the export of arms to both sides because of the fear of international complications. The embargo, as Day Lewis shows in the poem, was very keenly felt by the Government side.

The actual situation bears a strong resemblance to the fight of Sir Richard Grenville in the *Revenge* against the Spanish fleet, which is so magnificently described in Tennyson's poem *The Revenge: A Ballad of the Fleet*.

WELSH INCIDENT

'But that was nothing to what things came out
From the sea-caves of Criccieth yonder.'
'What were they? Mermaids? dragons? ghosts?'
'Nothing at all of any things like that.'
'What were they, then?' 'All sorts of queer things,
Things never seen or heard or written about,
Very strange, un-Welsh, utterly peculiar
Things. Oh, solid enough they seemed to touch,
Had anyone dared it. Marvellous creation,
All various shapes and sizes and no sizes,
All new, each perfectly unlike his neighbour,
Though all came moving slowly out together.'
'Describe just one of them.' 'I am unable.'
'What were their colours?' 'Mostly nameless colours,
Colours you'd like to see; but one was puce
Or perhaps more like crimson, but not purplish.
Some had no colour.' 'Tell me, had they legs?'
'Not a leg or foot among them that I saw.'
'But did these things come out in any order?
What o'clock was it? What was the day of the week?
Who else was present? What was the weather?'
'I was coming to that. It was half-past three
On Easter Tuesday last. The sun was shining.
The Harlech Silver Band played *Marchog Jesu*
On thirty-seven shimmering instruments,
Collecting for Carnarvon's (Fever) Hospital Fund.
The populations of Pwllheli, Criccieth,
Portmadoc, Borth, Tremadoc, Penrhyndeudraeth,
Were all assembled. Criccieth's mayor addressed them
First in good Welsh and then in fluent English,
Twisting his fingers in his chain of office,

Welcoming the things. They came out on the sand,
Not keeping time to the band, moving seaward
Silently at a snail's pace. But at last
The most odd, indescribable thing of all
Which hardly one man there could see for wonder
Did something recognisably a something.'
'Well, what?' 'It made a noise.' 'A frightening noise?'
'No, no.'
     'A musical noise? A noise of scuffling?'
'No, but a very loud, respectable noise—
Like groaning to oneself on Sunday morning
In Chapel, close before the second psalm.'
'What did the mayor do?' 'I was coming to that.'

                                    ROBERT GRAVES

Robert Graves (b. 1895), one of the finest poets of our time, is also well known for his *Good-Bye To All That*, a penetrating study of his childhood, early manhood and his experiences in the First World War, and also for his historical novels, of which the best known are *I, Claudius* and *Claudius the God*. He is a critic of great quality, a skilful broadcaster, and the author of several books of considerable scholarship but debatable conclusions.

As with *Flannan Isle*, but for a different reason, the solution of the mystery of *Welsh Incident* is happily omitted.

BALLAD

O what is that sound which so thrills the ear
  Down in the valley drumming, drumming?
Only the scarlet soldiers, dear,
  The soldiers coming.

O what is that light I see flashing so clear
  Over the distance brightly, brightly?
Only the sun on their weapons, dear,
  As they step lightly.

O what are they doing with all that gear;
  What are they doing this morning, this morning?
Only the usual manœuvres, dear,
  Or perhaps a warning.

O why have they left the road down there;
  Why are they suddenly wheeling, wheeling?
Perhaps a change in the orders, dear;
  Why are you kneeling?

O haven't they stopped for the doctor's care;
  Haven't they reined their horses, their horses?
Why, they are none of them wounded, dear,
  None of these forces.

O is it the parson they want with white hair;
  Is it the parson, is it, is it?
No, they are passing his gateway, dear,
  Without a visit.

O it must be the farmer who lives so near;
  It must be the farmer so cunning, so cunning ?
They have passed the farm already, dear,
    And now they are running.

O where are you going ? stay with me here!
  Were the vows you swore me deceiving, deceiving
No, I promised to love you, dear,
    But I must be leaving.

O it's broken the lock and splintered the door,
  O it's the gate where they're turning, turning;
Their feet are heavy on the floor
    And their eyes are burning.

                    W. H. AUDEN

Wystan Hugh Auden (1907–1973), like C. Day Lewis, first attracted attention in the 'thirties for the new note in his poetry. It has been said of him that 'no other poet of his generation can place beside his a body of work so exciting for its peculiar insight, its range of reference and its skill in the use of language and rhythm'.

Mr. Auden held the Professorship of Poetry at the University of Oxford from 1956 to 1961.

This poem suggests a comparison with the ballad *Edward* (p. 25). In both, the story is told through question and answer, the question in the first half and the answer in the second half of each verse, with a pattern of repetition, leading to the climax. But Auden's poem differs from *Edward* in its fascinating ambiguity and deliberate obscurity. We do not know why the soldiers have come, or whether they have come for the man or the woman, or what is the relationship between the two speakers. But there is a sinister implication throughout, in that one of the speakers is neither alarmed nor surprised at the arrival of the soldiers.

Part Three

EXTRACTS FROM LONGER NARRATIVE
POEMS

PARADISE LOST

From BOOK I

                             ... his pride
Had cast him out from Heav'n, with all his host
Of rebel angels, by whose aid aspiring
To set himself in glory above his peers,
He trusted to have equall'd the Most High,
If he oppos'd; and with ambitious aim
Against the throne and monarchy of God
Rais'd impious war in Heav'n, and battle proud
With vain attempt. Him the Almighty Power
Hurl'd headlong flaming from th' ethereal sky   10
With hideous ruin and combustion down
To bottomless perdition, there to dwell
In adamantine chains and penal fire,
Who durst defy th' Omnipotent to arms.
   Nine times the space that measures day and night
To mortal men, he with his horrid crew
Lay vanquisht, rolling in the fiery gulf,
Confounded though immortal: but his doom
Reserv'd him to more wrath; for now the thought
Both of lost happiness and lasting pain   20
Torments him: round he throws his baleful eyes
That witness'd huge affliction and dismay
Mixt with obdurate pride and stedfast hate.
At once as far as angels ken he views
The dismal situation waste and wild;
A dungeon horrible on all sides round
As one great furnace flam'd; yet from those flames
No light, but rather darkness visible

---

1 *his pride*—*his* refers to Satan, the fallen Angel.

Serv'd only to discover sights of woe,
Regions of sorrow, doleful shades, where peace   30
And rest can never dwell, hope never comes
That comes to all; but torture without end
Still urges, and a fiery deluge, fed
With ever-burning sulphur, unconsum'd:
Such place Eternal Justice had prepar'd
For those rebellious, here their prison ordain'd
In utter darkness, and their portion set
As far remov'd from God and light of Heav'n
As from the centre thrice to th' utmost pole.
O how unlike the place from whence they fell!   40
There the companions of his fall, o'erwhelm'd
With floods and whirlwinds of tempestuous fire,
He soon discerns; and welt'ring by his side
One next himself in power, and next in crime,
Long after known in Palestine, and nam'd
Beëlzebub. To whom th' Arch-Enemy,
And thence in Heav'n call'd Satan, with bold words
Breaking the horrid silence thus began.

'If thou beest he; but O how fall'n! how chang'd
From him, who in the happy realms of light   50
Cloth'd with transcendent brightness didst outshine
Myriads though bright: if he whom mutual league,
United thoughts and counsels, equal hope
And hazard in the glorious enterprise,
Join'd with me once, now misery hath join'd
In equal ruin: into what pit thou seest
From what highth fall'n; so much the stronger prov'd
He with his thunder: and till then who knew
The force of those dire arms? Yet not for those,
Nor what the potent Victor in his rage   60
Can else inflict, do I repent or change
(Though chang'd in outward lustre) that fixt mind,

46 *Beëlzebub*—'Lord of Flies', worshipped in Ekron, a city of Palestine infested with
flies against which the protection of the god was invoked. See *Matt.* xii. 24.

And high disdain from sense of injur'd merit,
That with the Mightiest rais'd me to contend,
And to the fierce contention brought along
Innumerable force of spirits arm'd
That durst dislike his reign, and me preferring,
His utmost power with adverse power oppos'd
In dubious battle on the plains of Heav'n,
And shook his throne. What though the field be lost?   70
All is not lost; the unconquerable will,
And study of revenge, immortal hate,
And courage never to submit or yield,
And what is else not to be overcome;
That glory never shall his wrath or might
Extort from me. To bow and sue for grace
With suppliant knee, and deify his power,
Who from the terror of this arm so late
Doubted his empire, that were low indeed,
That were an ignominy and shame beneath   80
This downfall; since by fate the strength of gods
And this empyreal substance cannot fail,
Since through experience of this great event
In arms not worse, in foresight much advanc't,
We may with more successful hope resolve
To wage by force or guile eternal war,
Irreconcilable to our grand Foe
Who now triumphs, and in th' excess of joy
Sole reigning holds the tyranny of Heav'n.'

  So spake th' apostate Angel, though in pain,   90
Vaunting aloud, but rackt with deep despair:
And him thus answer'd soon his bold compeer.
'O Prince, O chief of many throned Powers,
That led th' imbattled seraphim to war
Under thy conduct, and in dreadful deeds
Fearless, endanger'd Heav'ns perpetual King;
And put to proof his high supremacy,
Whether upheld by strength, or chance, or fate;

Too well I see and rue the dire event,
That with sad overthrow and foul defeat   100
Hath lost us Heav'n, and all this mighty host
In horrible destruction laid thus low,
As far as gods and Heav'nly essences
Can perish: for the mind and spirit remains
Invincible, and vigour soon returns,
Though all our glory extinct, and happy state
Here swallow'd up in endless misery.
But what if he our Conqueror (whom I now
Of force believe Almighty, since no less
Than such could have o'er-pow'rd such force as ours)   110
Have left us this our spirit and strength entire
Strongly to suffer and support our pains,
That we may so suffice his vengeful ire,
Or do him mightier service as his thralls
By right of war, whate'er his business be,
Here in the heart of Hell to work in fire,
Or do his errands in the gloomy deep?
What can it then avail though yet we feel
Strength undiminisht, or eternal being
To undergo eternal punishment?'   120
    Whereto with speedy words th' Arch-Fiend reply'd.
'Fall'n cherub, to be weak is miserable,
Doing or suffering: but of this be sure,
To do aught good never will be our task,
But ever to do ill our sole delight,
As being the contrary to his high will
Whom we resist. If then his providence
Out of our evil seek to bring forth good,
Our labour must be to pervert that end,
And out of good still to find means of evil;   130
Which oft-times may succeed, so as perhaps
Shall grieve him, if I fail not, and disturb
His inmost counsels from their destin'd aim.
But see! the angry Victor hath recall'd

His ministers of vengeance and pursuit
Back to the gates of Heav'n; the sulphurous hail
Shot after us in storm, o'erblown, hath laid
The fiery surge, that from the precipice
Of Heav'n receiv'd us falling; and the thunder,
Wing'd with red lightning and impetuous rage,   140
Perhaps hath spent his shafts, and ceases now
To bellow through the vast and boundless deep.
Let us not slip th' occasion, whether scorn
Or satiate fury yield it from our Foe.
Seest thou yon dreary plain, forlorn and wild,
The seat of desolation, void of light,
Save what the glimmering of these livid flames
Casts pale and dreadful? Thither let us tend
From off the tossing of these fiery waves,
There rest, if any rest can harbour there,   150
And re-assembling our afflicted powers,
Consult how we may henceforth most offend
Our Enemy, our own loss how repair,
How overcome this dire calamity,
What reinforcement we may gain from hope,
If not what resolution from despair.'
    Thus Satan talking to his nearest mate
With head uplift above the nearest wave, and eyes
That sparkling blaz'd; his other parts besides
Prone on the flood, extended long and large,   160
Lay floating many a rood; in bulk as huge
As whom the fables name of monstrous size,
Titanian, or Earth-born, that warr'd on Jove,
Briareos or Typhon, whom the den
By ancient Tarsus held; or that sea-beast
Leviathan, which God of all his works
Created hugest that swim th' ocean stream;

163 *Titanian*—the Titans were the sons and daughters of heaven and earth, according
to Greek mythology. Jove (Jupiter) defeated them and became the supreme god. Typhon
was a Titan. Briareos, a hundred-handed giant, assisted Jupiter against the Titans.
166 *Leviathan*—the whale. See Book of *Job*, Chap. xl.

Him haply slumb'ring on the Norway foam,
The pilot of some small night-founder'd skiff
Deeming some island, oft, as seamen tell,   170
With fixed anchor in his scaly rind
Moors by his side under the lee, while night
Invests the sea, and wished morn delays:
So stretcht out huge in length the Arch-Fiend lay
Chain'd on the burning lake; nor ever thence
Had ris'n or heav'd his head, but that the will
And high permission of all-ruling Heaven
Left him at large to his own dark designs;
That with reiterated crimes he might
Heap on himself damnation, while he sought   180
Evil to others; and enrag'd might see
How all his malice serv'd but to bring forth
Infinite goodness, grace and mercy shown
On man by him seduc't; but on himself
Treble confusion, wrath and vengeance pour'd.
    Forthwith upright he rears from off the pool
His mighty stature; on each hand the flames
Driv'n backward slope their pointing spires, and roll'd
In billows, leave i' the midst a horrid vale.
Then with expanded wings he steers his flight   190
Aloft, incumbent on the dusky air
That felt unusual weight, till on dry land
He lights; if it were land that ever burn'd
With solid, as the lake with liquid fire,
And such appear'd in hue, as when the force
Of subterranean wind transports a hill
Torn from Pelorus, or the shatter'd side
Of thundr'ing Aetna, whose combustible
And fuell'd entrails thence conceiving fire,
Sublim'd with mineral fury, aid the winds,   200
And leave a singed bottom all involv'd
With stench and smoke: such resting found the sole

197 *Pelorus*—the north-east point of Sicily. Etna is a volcano in Sicily.

Of unblest feet. Him follow'd his next mate,
Both glorying to have scap't the Stygian flood
As gods, and by their own recover'd strength,
Not by the sufferance of supernal Power.
   'Is this the region, this the soil, the clime,'
Said then the lost Archangel; 'this the seat
That we must change for Heav'n? this mournful gloom
For that celestial light? Be it so, since he   210
Who now is Sovran can dispose and bid
What shall be right: farthest from him is best,
Whom reason hath equall'd, force hath made supreme
Above his equals. Farewell happy fields
Where joy for ever dwells: hail horrors, hail
Infernal world, and thou profoundest Hell
Receive thy new possessor; one who brings
A mind not to be chang'd by place or time.
The mind is its own place, and in itself
Can make a Heav'n of Hell, a Hell of Heav'n.   220
What matter where, if I be still the same,
And what I should be, all but less than he
Whom thunder hath made greater? Here at least
We shall be free; th' Almighty hath not built
Here for his envy, will not drive us hence:
Here we may reign secure, and in my choice
To reign is worth ambition though in Hell:
Better to reign in Hell than serve in Heav'n.
But wherefore let we then our faithful friends,
Th'associates and co-partners of our loss,   230
Lie thus astonish'd on th' oblivious pool,
And call them not to share with us their part
In this unhappy mansion, or once more
With rallied arms to try what may be yet
Regain'd in Heav'n, or what more lost in Hell?'
   So Satan spake, and him Beëlzebub
Thus answer'd. 'Leader of those armies bright,
Which but th' Omnipotent none could have foil'd,

If once they hear that voice, their liveliest pledge
Of hope in fears and dangers, heard so oft   240
In worst extremes, and on the perilous edge
Of battle when it rag'd, in all assaults
Their surest signal, they will soon resume
New courage and revive, though now they lie
Groveling and prostrate on yon lake of fire,
As we erewhile, astounded and amaz'd;
No wonder, fall'n such a pernicious highth.'
    He scarce had ceas'd when the superior Fiend
Was moving toward the shore; his ponderous shield
Ethereal temper, massy, large and round,   250
Behind him cast; the broad circumference
Hung on his shoulders like the moon, whose orb
Through optic glass the Tuscan artist views
At ev'ning from the top of Fesolè,
Or in Val d'Arno, to descry new lands,
Rivers or mountains in her spotty globe.
His spear, to equal which the tallest pine
Hewn on Norwegian hills, to be the mast
Of some great ammiral, were but a wand,
He walkt with to support uneasy steps   260
Over the burning marle, not like those steps
On Heav'ns azure; and the torrid clime
Smote on him sore besides, vaulted with fire:
Nathless he so endur'd, till on the beach
Of that inflamed sea, he stood and call'd
His legions, angel forms, who lay entranct
Thick as autumnal leaves that strow the brooks
In Vallombrosa, where th' Etrurian shades
High over-arch't imbowr; or scattered sedge

253 *The Tuscan artist*—Galileo (1564-1642) with his newly invented telescope was able to 'explore' the surface of the moon. *Fesole* is a village near Florence, the Val d'Arno the valley of the River Arno, in which Florence lies.
259 *ammiral*—the principal vessel in the fleet.
268 *Vallombrosa*—eighteen miles from Florence, and thickly wooded.

Afloat, when with fierce winds Orion arm'd   270
Hath vext the Red-Sea coast, whose waves o'erthrew
Busiris and his Memphian chivalry,
While with perfidious hatred they pursu'd
The sojourners of Goshen, who beheld
From the same shore their floating carcasses
And broken chariot-wheels; so thick bestrown
Abject and lost lay these, covering the flood,
Under amazement of their hideous change.
He call'd so loud, that all the hollow deep
Of Hell resounded: 'Princes, Potentates,   280
Warriors, the flow'r of Heav'n, once yours, now lost,
If such astonishment as this can seize
Eternal spirits; or have ye chos'n this place
After the toil of battle to repose
Your wearied virtue, for the ease you find
To slumber here, as in the vales of Heav'n?
Or in this abject posture have ye sworn
To adore the Conqueror? who now beholds
Cherub and seraph rolling in the flood
With scatter'd arms and ensigns, till anon   290
His swift pursuers from Heav'n-gates discern
Th' advantage; and descending tread us down
Thus drooping, or with linked thunderbolts
Transfix us to the bottom of this gulf.
Awake, arise, or be for ever fall'n.'
      They heard, and were abasht, and up they sprung
Upon the wing; as when men wont to watch
On duty sleeping found by whom they dread,
Rouse and bestir themselves ere well awake.
Nor did they not perceive the evil plight   300
In which they were, or the fierce pains not feel;

270 *Orion*—a mighty hunter who, at his death, according to the myth, was placed
among the stars. His setting, in November, is a time of fierce storms. *Busiris of Memphis*
is the name given by Milton to the Pharaoh who with his army was lost in the Red Sea
when pursuing the Hebrews. See *Exodus* xiv. 30.

Yet to their general's voice they soon obey'd
Innumerable. As when the potent rod
Of Amram's son in Egypt's evil day
Wav'd round the coast, up call'd a pitchy cloud
Of locusts, warping on the eastern wind,
That o'er the realm of impious Pharaoh hung
Like night, and darken'd all the land of Nile:
So numberless were those bad angels seen
Hovering on wing under the cope of Hell   310
'Twixt upper, nether, and surrounding fires;
Till, as a signal giv'n, th' uplifted spear
Of their great sultan waving to direct
Their course, in even balance down they light
On the firm brimstone, and fill all the plain;
A multitude, like which the populous North
Pour'd never from her frozen loins, to pass
Rhene or the Danaw; when her barbarous sons
Came like a deluge on the South, and spread
Beneath Gibraltar to the Libyan sands.   320
Forthwith from every squadron and each band
The heads and leaders thither haste where stood
Their great commander; godlike shapes and forms
Excelling human, princely Dignities,
And Powers that erst in Heav'n sat on thrones;
Though of their names in Heav'ns records now
Be no memorial, blotted out and ras'd
By their rebellion from the books of life.

JOHN MILTON

303 *the potent rod* . . . these lines refer to the plague of locusts which Moses called up
over Egypt when Pharaoh refused to release the Hebrews.

318 *her barbarous sons* . . . the fallen angels are compared with the hordes of the Vandal
tribes who burst into southern Europe, ravaged through Spain and settled finally in
Northern Africa.

John Milton (1608–1674) is generally regarded as our greatest poet after Shakespeare. Few men have been so dedicated to poetry, for even in youth he had dedicated himself, and spent most of his early manhood in an arduous training through reading, scholarship and the practice of poetry. His early work (written before the Civil War) would alone have established his reputation: *L'Allegro, Il Penseroso, Lycidas, Arcades* and *Comus*. During the troubled period of the Civil War, his chief work was the writing of political pamphlets, a work which he continued when appointed Latin Secretary to the Government of the Protectorate. Some of these pamphlets, in particular *Areopagitica* in defence of the freedom of the Press, established him as one of our greatest prose-writers. After the Restoration, blind, poor and obscure, he wrote *Paradise Lost, Paradise Regained* and *Samson Agonistes*, three of the most sublime poems in English.

In *Paradise Lost* Milton attempted, in his own words, to 'justify the ways of God to men'. It narrates the rebellion in Heaven of Satan against God, Satan's defeat, God's creation of Man and the Fall of Man.

This extract describes the first recovery of Satan and the defeated angels after being flung into Hell. Much of Milton's conception of Hell and of Heaven is too literal and physical to be accepted by the modern mind. For example, we do not think of Satan in physical terms as a colossal giant. But this does not prevent us from accepting in the imagination this mighty story.

Few poets have been so saturated with the Bible and classical literature. He turns, almost in second nature, to the Bible, to the myths and literature of Greece and Rome for his illustrations and comparisons. Notice his frequent use of the epic simile (cp. *Sohrab and Rustum*). It was through this type of imagery, above all, that he was able to depict in concrete terms a war of spirits otherwise indescribable in human language.

Milton's creation of Satan is penetrating and awe-inspiring. It has been claimed that Milton could write of him with intuitive sympathy because he himself was always a rebel against spiritual authoritarianism. 'Milton,' said William Blake, 'was of the Devil's party without knowing it.'

SAMSON AGONISTES

The Death of Samson

Occasions drew me early to this city;
And as the gates I enter'd with sun-rise,
The morning trumpets festival proclaim'd
Through each high street: little I had dispatch't,
When all abroad was rumour'd that this day
Samson should be brought forth to show the people
Proof of his mighty strength in feats and games;
I sorrow'd at his captive state, but minded
Not to be absent at that spectacle.
The building was a spacious theatre   10
Half-round, on two main pillars vaulted high,
With seats where all the lords, and each degree
Of sort, might sit in order to behold;
The other side was op'n, where the throng
On banks and scaffolds under sky might stand;
I among these aloof obscurely stood.
The feast and noon grew high, and sacrifice
Had fill'd their hearts with mirth, high cheer, and wine,
When to their sports they turn'd. Immediately
Was Samson as a public servant brought,   20
In their state livery clad; before him pipes
And timbrels, on each side went armed guards,
Both horse and foot before him and behind,
Archers, and slingers, cataphracts and spears.
At sight of him the people with a shout
Rifted the air, clamouring their god with praise,
Who had made their dreadful enemy their thrall.
He patient but undaunted where they led him,
Came to the place, and what was set before him

22 *timbrel*—tambourine.
24 *cataphract*—heavy-armed cavalry, with both horses and riders armoured.

Which without help of eye, might be assay'd,   30
To heave, pull, draw, or break, he still perform'd
All with incredible, stupendious force,
None daring to appear antagonist.
At length for intermission sake they led him
Between the pillars; he his guide requested,
(For so from such as nearer stood we heard)
As over-tir'd, to let him lean a while
With both his arms on those two massy pillars
That to the arched roof gave main support.
He unsuspicious led him; which when Samson   40
Felt in his arms, with head a while inclin'd,
And eyes fast fixt he stood, as one who pray'd,
Or some great matter in his mind revolv'd.
At last with head erect thus cri'd aloud.
'Hitherto, lords, what your commands impos'd
I have perform'd, as reason was, obeying,
Not without wonder or delight beheld.
Now of my own accord such other trial
I mean to show you of my strength, yet greater,
As with amaze shall strike all who behold.'   50
This utter'd, straining all his nerves he bow'd;
As with the force of winds and waters pent,
When mountains tremble, those two massy pillars
With horrible convulsion to and fro
He tugg'd, he shook, till down they came and drew
The whole roof after them, with burst of thunder
Upon the heads of all who sat beneath,
Lords, ladies, captains, counsellors, or priests,
Their choice nobility and flower, not only
Of this, but each Philistian city round,   60
Met from all parts to solemnise this feast.
Samson with these immixt, inevitably
Pull'd down the same destruction on himself;
The vulgar only 'scap'd who stood without.

                                        JOHN MILTON

The story of Samson is to be found in the Book of *Judges*, xiii–xiv. This passage is from Milton's tragedy, *Samson Agonistes*. The play conforms very closely to the practice of Greek classical tragedy and was not intended for production on the stage. The scene throughout is set in the Philistine prison during the last hour or so of Samson's life. Towards the end Samson leaves the stage to display his strength before the assembled Philistines, and the 'Messenger' returns to report his death and triumph. The verse is more direct and less ornate than that of *Paradise Lost*.

THE RAPE OF THE LOCK

Canto III

Close by those meads, for ever crown'd with flow'rs,
Where Thames with pride surveys his rising tow'rs,
There stands a structure of majestic frame,
Which from the neighb'ring Hampton takes its name.
Here Britain's statesmen oft the fall foredoom
Of foreign Tyrants, and of Nymphs at home;
Here thou, great ANNA! whom three realms obey,
Dost sometimes counsel take—and sometimes Tea.
Hither the Heroes and the Nymphs resort,
To taste awhile the pleasures of a Court;   10
In various talk th' instructive hours they past,
Who gave the ball, or paid the visit last;
One speaks the glory of the British Queen,
And one describes a charming Indian screen;
A third interprets motions, looks and eyes;
At ev'ry word a reputation dies.
Snuff, or the fan, supply each pause of chat,
With singing, laughing, ogling, *and all that.*
    Mean while, declining from the noon of day,
The sun obliquely shoots his burning ray;   20
The hungry Judges soon the sentence sign,
And wretches hang that Jury-men may dine;
The merchant from th' Exchange returns in peace,
And the long labours of the Toilet cease.
Belinda now, whom thirst of fame invites,
Burns to encounter two advent'rous Knights,
At Ombre singly to decide their doom;

---

27 *Ombre*—The game was played with forty cards of the standard pack, the 8s, 9s and 10s being discarded. The three players each took a hand of nine cards, and the remaining cards went into a kind of pool. There were three principal trumps, called *Matadores:*

And swells her breast with conquests yet to come.
Straight the three bands prepare in arms to join,
Each band the number of the sacred Nine.   30
Soon as she spreads her hand, th' aërial guard
Descend, and sit on each important card:
First Ariel perch'd upon a Matadore,
Then each according to the rank they bore;
For Sylphs, yet mindful of their ancient race,
Are, as when women, wond'rous fond of place.

Behold, four Kings in majesty rever'd,
With hoary whiskers and a forky beard;
And four fair Queens whose hands sustain a flow'r,
Th' expressive emblem of their softer pow'r;   40
Four Knaves in garbs succinct, a trusty band,
Caps on their heads, and halberts in their hand;
And particolour'd troops, a shining train,
Draw forth to combat on the velvet plain.

The skilful Nymph reviews her force with care:
'Let Spades be trumps!' she said, and trumps they were.

Now move to war her sable Matadores,
In show like leaders of the swarthy Moors.
Spadillio first, unconquerable Lord!
Led off two captive trumps, and swept the board.   50
As many more Manillio forc'd to yield,
And march'd a victor from the verdant field.

Spadille, the Ace of Spades: *Basto*, the Ace of Clubs: and *Manille*, the second trump at
Ombre, the Two of Spades, when Spades are trumps. In the game played by Belinda,
Spades are trumps.

Readers might be interested to see how the game worked out:

Belinda: Ace Spades (*Spadille*), 2 of Spades (*Manille*), Ace Clubs (*Basto*), King
Spades, King Clubs, King Hearts, Queen Hearts, 3 of Diamonds,
2 of Diamonds.

Baron: Queen Spades, Knave Spades, 6 of Spades, 5 of Spades, 4 of Spades
King Diamonds, Queen Diamonds, Knave Diamonds, Ace Hearts.

The Dealer: 3 of Spades, 7 of Spades, Knave Clubs, 2 of Clubs, Knave Hearts, 6
of Hearts, 4 of Hearts, 3 of Hearts, 2 of Hearts.

Belinda wins the first four tricks, the Baron the next four, and then Belinda wins the final
trick with her King of Hearts, which beats the Baron's Ace of Hearts because the Ace of
Hearts ranks below the Knave when Clubs or Spades are trumps. Hence Belinda's King
of Hearts 'falls like thunder on the prostrate Ace'.

Him Basto follow'd, but his fate more hard
Gain'd but one trump and one Plebeian card.
With his broad sabre next, a chief in years,
The hoary Majesty of Spades appears,
Puts forth one manly leg, to sight reveal'd,
The rest, his many-colour'd robe conceal'd.
The rebel Knave, who dares his prince engage,
Proves the just victim of his royal rage.   60
Ev'n mighty Pam, that Kings and Queens o'erthrew
And mow'd down armies in the fights of Loo,
Sad chance of war! now destitute of aid,
Falls undistinguish'd by the victor Spade!
Thus far both armies to Belinda yield;
Now to the Baron fate inclines the field.
His warlike Amazon her host invades,
Th' imperial consort of the crown of Spades.
The Club's black Tyrant first her victim dy'd,
Spite of his haughty mien, and barb'rous pride: 70
What boots the regal circle on his head,
His giant limbs, in state unwieldy spread;
That long behind he trails his pompous robe,
And, of all monarchs, only grasps the globe?
    The Baron now his Diamonds pours apace;
Th' embroider'd King who shows but half his face,
And his refulgent Queen, with pow'rs combin'd,
Of broken troops, an easy conquest find.
Clubs, Diamonds, Hearts, in wild disorder seen,
With throngs promiscuous strow the level green.   80
Thus when dispers'd a routed army runs,
Of Asia's troops, and Afric's sable sons,
With like confusion different nations fly,
Of various habit and of various dye;
The pierc'd battalions disunited fall,
In heaps on heaps; one fate o'erwhelms them all.
    The Knave of Diamonds tries his wily arts,

61 *Pam*—Knave of Clubs, the highest card in the game of Loo.

And wins (oh shameful chance!) the Queen of Hearts.
At this, the blood the virgin's cheek forsook,
A livid paleness spreads o'er all her look;   90
She sees, and trembles at th' approaching ill,
Just in the jaws of ruin, and Codille.
And now (as oft in some distemper'd State)
On one nice Trick depends the gen'ral fate:
An Ace of Hearts steps forth: the King unseen
Lurk'd in her hand, and mourn'd his captive Queen:
He springs to vengeance with an eager pace,
And falls like thunder on the prostrate Ace.
The nymph, exulting, fills with shouts the sky;
The walls, the woods, and long canals reply.   100
    O thoughtless mortals! ever blind to fate,
Too soon dejected, and too soon elate.
Sudden these honours shall be snatch'd away,
And curs'd for ever this victorious day.
    For lo! the board with cups and spoons is crown'd,
The berries crackle, and the mill turns round;
On shining altars of Japan they raise
The silver lamp; the fiery spirits blaze:
From silver spouts the grateful liquors glide,
While China's earth receives the smoking tide: 110
At once they gratify their sense and taste,
And frequent cups prolong the rich repast.
Straight hover round the Fair her airy band;
Some, as she sipp'd, the fuming liquor fann'd,
Some o'er her lap their careful plumes display'd,
Trembling, and conscious of the rich brocade.
Coffee (which makes the politician wise,
And see through all things with his half-shut eyes)
Sent up in vapours to the Baron's brain
New stratagems, the radiant Lock to gain.   120
Ah cease, rash youth! desist ere 'tis too late,

92 *Codille*—the loss of the game.
106 *berries*—coffee, an extremely fashionable drink at the time.

Fear the just Gods, and think of Scylla's Fate!
Chang'd to a bird, and sent to flit in air,
She dearly pays for Nisus' injur'd hair!
　　But when to mischief mortals bend their will,
How soon they find fit instruments of ill ?
Just then, Clarissa drew with tempting grace
A two-edg'd weapon from her shining case:
So Ladies in Romance assist their Knight,
Present the spear, and arm him for the fight.   130
He takes the gift with rev'rence, and extends
The little engine on his fingers' ends;
This just behind Belinda's neck he spread,
As o'er the fragrant steams she bends her head.
Swift to the Lock a thousand Sprites repair,
A thousand wings, by turns, blow back the hair;
And thrice they twitch'd the diamond in her ear;
Thrice she look'd back, and thrice the foe drew near.
Just in that instant, anxious Ariel sought
The close recesses of the Virgin's thought;   140
As on the nosegay in her breast reclin'd,
He watch'd th' ideas rising in her mind,
Sudden he view'd, in spite of all her art,
An earthly Lover lurking at her heart.
Amaz'd, confus'd, he found his pow'r expir'd,
Resign'd to fate, and with a sigh retir'd.
The Peer now spreads the glitt'ring Forfex wide,
T' inclose the Lock; now joins it, to divide.
Ev'n then, before the fatal engine clos'd,
A wretched Sylph too fondly interpos'd;   150
Fate urg'd the shears, and cut the Sylph in twain,
(But airy substance soon unites again)

122 *Scylla*—daughter of Nisus, King of Megara. In love with Minos, who was besieging her father's city, she pulled out her father's golden hair, on which his life depended. Minos, disgusted by her unnatural conduct, threw her into the sea, but she was metamorphosed into a bird.
147 *Forfex* (Latin)—scissors.
151 *cut the Sylph*—a sly glance at *Paradise Lost*, in which the Angel Michael cut Satan in two, but Satan, being immortal, was reunited.

The meeting points the sacred hair dissever
From the fair head, for ever, and for ever !
Then flash'd the living lightning from her eyes,
And screams of horror rend th' affrighted skies.
Not louder shrieks to pitying heav'n are cast,
When husbands, or when lapdogs breathe their last;
Or when rich China vessels fall'n from high,
In glitt'ring dust and painted fragments lie !   160
    Let wreaths of triumph now my temples twine,
(The victor cry'd) the glorious prize is mine !
While fish in streams, or birds delight in air,
Or in a coach and six the British Fair,
As long as Atalantis shall be read,
Or the small pillow grace a Lady's bed,
While visits shall be paid on solemn days,
When num'rous wax-lights in bright order blaze,
While nymphs take treats, or assignations give,
So long my honour, name and praise shall live !   170
What Time would spare, from Steel receives its date,
And monuments, like men, submit to fate !
Steel could the labour of the Gods destroy,
And strike to dust th' imperial tow'rs of Troy;
Steel could the works of mortal pride confound,
And hew triumphal arches to the ground.
What wonder then, fair nymph ! thy hairs should feel,
The conqu'ring force of unresisted steel ?

ALEXANDER POPE

165 *Atalantis*—a loose and scandalous romance which, it has been said, 'well suited the debauched taste of the better vulgar', by Mrs. Manley (1683–1724).

Alexander Pope (1688–1744) was an outstanding personality in literary and social circles in the early eighteenth century, and of profound influence in setting standards of literary taste which lasted until after the turn of the next century. Apart from his translations, his poetry is chiefly moral, semi-philosophical or satirical. Although he never lost his reputation for superb technique and pungent satire, many nineteenth-century critics denied him merit as a poet. For example, Matthew Arnold says that he is 'the high priest of an age of prose and reason', and that his poetry is 'the poetry of the builders of an age of prose and reason'. Neither statement seems to have much meaning to-day, when Pope is increasingly recognised as a true, original and great poet.

The incident which gave rise to *The Rape of The Lock* was a trivial one which created an exaggerated stir in high Catholic society. Miss Arabella Fermor (the *Belinda* of the poem), a celebrated beauty of the day, had one of her curls snipped off by Lord Petre. Relations between the two families became greatly strained, and it was suggested to Pope that a light-hearted treatment of the triviality by a Catholic poet would help to put the incident in the right perspective. The first version of the poem was in two cantos only, and published without the author's name, although the authorship was no secret. The later version, in five cantos, was much more elaborate. The poem delighted everyone except the Baron (Sir George Brown of Kiddington) and Miss Fermor's family. Miss Fermor herself seems to have changed her mind. In a letter to his friend Caryll, who had suggested the idea, Pope wrote that 'the celebrated lady herself is offended', but William Warburton, Pope's literary executor, who brought out an edition of Pope's works in 1751, wrote that 'she took it so well as to give about copies of it'.

The poem is a mock-epic, with all the 'machinery' of attendant divinities (*Sylphs*) watching over their human favourites in a contest wittily dignified with the epic importance of the siege of Troy. It is not, however, merely a witty parody or delightful *jeu d'esprit*. As Professor Grant says in the preface to the *Penguin* selection of the poetry of Pope:

> 'The poem is heroic poetry refined until murmurs of the war for Helen, the strife of Hector and Achilles on the sun-baked plain before Troy, and the clanging of Rinaldo's bright armour, sound under the shady trees in Hampton Court and in the airs that breathe around Belinda. The continual suggestion of heroic verse dignifies the quarrel over the lock and, at the same time, so risible is the comparison of great and small, invests it with humour. . . . When the lock has been severed by the scissors, the poet movingly exclaims:
>
>> What Time would spare, from Steel receives its date,
>> And monuments, like men, submit to fate!

This is no mere lamentation over a lock of hair; it is a gentle but passionate cry over all beauty wantonly destroyed. These implications that underlie the poem give it strength, and, saving it from drawing-room comedy, translate it into an "echo of divine music".'

THE PRELUDE, BOOK I

Episodes from the Childhood of Wordsworth

One summer evening (led by her) I found
A little boat tied to a willow tree
Within a rocky cave, its usual home.
Straight I unloosed her chain, and stepping in
Pushed from the shore. It was an act of stealth
And troubled pleasure, nor without the voice
Of mountain-echoes did my boat move on;
Leaving behind her still, on either side,
Small circles glittering idly in the moon,
Until they melted all into one track   10
Of sparkling light. But now, like one who rows,
Proud of his skill, to reach a chosen point
With an unswerving line, I fixed my view
Upon the summit of a craggy ridge,
The horizon's utmost boundary; far above
Was nothing but the stars and the grey sky.
She was an elfin pinnace; lustily
I dipped my oars into the silent lake,
And, as I rose upon the stroke, my boat
Went heaving through the water like a swan;   20
When, from behind that craggy steep till then
The horizon's bound, a huge peak, black and huge,
As if with voluntary power instinct
Upreared its head. I struck and struck again,
And growing still in stature the grim shape
Towered up between me and the stars, and still,
For so it seemed, with purpose of its own
And measured motion like a living thing,
Strode after me. With trembling oars I turned,
And through the silent water stole my way   30

Back to the covert of the willow tree;
There in her mooring-place I left my bark,—
And through the meadows homeward went, in grave
And serious mood; but after I had seen
That spectacle, for many days, my brain
Worked with a dim and undetermined sense
Of unknown modes of being; o'er my thoughts
There hung a darkness, call it solitude
Or blank desertion. No familiar shapes
Remained, no pleasant images of trees,   40
Of sea or sky, no colours of green fields;
But huge and mighty forms, that do not live
Like living men, moved slowly through the mind
By day, and were a trouble to my dreams.

    Wisdom and Spirit of the universe!
Thou Soul that art the eternity of thought,
That givest to forms and images a breath
And everlasting motion, not in vain
By day or star-light thus from my first dawn
Of childhood didst thou intertwine for me   50
The passions that build up our human soul;
Not with the mean and vulgar works of man,
But with high objects, with enduring things—
With life and nature—purifying thus
The elements of feeling and of thought,
And sanctifying, by such discipline,
Both pain and fear, until we recognise
A grandeur in the beatings of the heart.
Nor was this fellowship vouchsafed to me
With stinted kindness. In November days,   60
When vapours rolling down the valley made
A lonely scene more lonesome, among woods,
At noon and 'mid the calm of summer nights,
When, by the margin of the trembling lake,
Beneath the gloomy hills homeward I went

In solitude, such intercourse was mine;
Mine was it in the fields both day and night,
And by the waters, all the summer long.

And in the frosty season, when the sun
Was set, and visible for many a mile   70
The cottage windows blazed through twilight gloom,
I heeded not their summons: happy time
It was indeed for all of us—for me
It was a time of rapture! Clear and loud
The village clock tolled six,—I wheeled about,
Proud and exulting like an untired horse
That cares not for his home. All shod with steel,
We hissed along the polished ice in games
Confederate, imitative of the chase
And woodland pleasures,—the resounding horn,   80
The pack loud chiming, and the hunted hare.
So through the darkness and the cold we flew,
And not a voice was idle; with the din
Smitten, the precipices rang aloud;
The leafless trees and every icy crag
Tinkled like iron; while far distant hills
Into the tumult sent an alien sound
Of melancholy not unnoticed, while the stars
Eastward were sparkling clear, and in the west
The orange sky of evening died away.   90
Not seldom from the uproar I retired
Into a silent bay, or sportively
Glanced sideway, leaving the tumultuous throng,
To cut across the reflex of a star
That fled, and, flying still before me, gleamed
Upon the glassy plain; and oftentimes,
When we had given our bodies to the wind,
And all the shadowy banks on either side
Came sweeping through the darkness, spinning still
The rapid line of motion, then at once   100

Have I, reclining back upon my heels,
Stopped short; yet still the solitary cliffs
Wheeled by me—even as if the earth had rolled
With visible motion her diurnal round!
Behind me did they stretch in solemn train,
Feebler and feebler, and I stood and watched
Till all was tranquil as a dreamless sleep.

WILLIAM WORDSWORTH

It was Wordsworth's ambition to write a great philosophical poem, and in preparation for this he composed *The Prelude or Growth of a Poet's Mind*, written between 1799 and 1805, but not published until 1850. The following is an extract from the Preface:

> Several years ago, when the Author retired to his native mountains with the hope of being enabled to construct a literary work that might live, it was a reasonable thing that he should take a review of his own mind, and examine how far Nature and Education had qualified him for such an employment.
> As subsidiary to this preparation, he undertook to record, in verse, the origin and progress of his own powers, as far as he was acquainted with them. . . .
> The preparatory poem is biographical, and conducts the history of the Author's mind to the point when he was emboldened to hope that his faculties were sufficiently matured for entering upon the arduous labour which he had proposed to himself.

The Prelude, a far finer poem than the great work which he hoped to achieve, is a long poem of fourteen books, in which Wordsworth describes and analyses his intellectual and spiritual development from childhood to manhood. Even in the boyhood activities so memorably described in this extract, Wordsworth the man sees a profound spiritual significance.

HYPERION

BOOK I

Deep in the shady sadness of a vale
Far sunken from the healthy breath of morn,
Far from the fiery noon, and eve's one star,
Sat grey-hair'd Saturn, quiet as a stone,
Still as the silence round about his lair;
Forest on forest hung about his head
Like cloud on cloud. No stir of air was there,
Not so much life as on a summer's day
Robs not one light seed from the feather'd grass,
But where the dead leaf fell, there did it rest.   10
A stream went voiceless by, still deadened more
By reason of his fallen divinity
Spreading a shade: the Naiad 'mid her reeds
Press'd her cold finger closer to her lips.

Along the margin-sand large foot-marks went,
No further than to where his feet had stray'd,
And slept there since. Upon the sodden ground
His old right hand lay nerveless, listless, dead,
Unsceptred; and his realmless eyes were closed;
While his bow'd head seemed list'ning to the Earth,   20
His ancient mother, for some comfort yet.

It seem'd no force could wake him from his place;
But there came one, who with a kindred hand
Touch'd his wide shoulders, after bending low
With reverence, though to one who knew it not.

---

13 *Naiad*—the *Naiades*, in Greek mythology, were the lesser divinities who guarded rivers, lakes and springs.

She was a goddess of the infant world;
By her in stature the tall Amazon
Had stood a pigmy's height: she would have ta'en
Achilles by the hair and bent his neck;
Or with a finger stay'd Ixion's wheel.   30
Her face was large as that of Memphian sphinx,
Pedestal'd haply in a palace court,
When sages look'd to Egypt for their lore.
But oh! how unlike marble was that face:
How beautiful, if sorrow had not made
Sorrow more beautiful than Beauty's self.
There was a listening fear in her regard,
As if calamity had but begun;
As if the vanward clouds of evil days
Had spent their malice, and the sullen rear   40
Was with its stored thunder labouring up.
One hand she press'd upon that aching spot
Where beats the human heart, as if just there,
Though an immortal, she felt cruel pain:
The other upon Saturn's bended neck
She laid, and to the level of his ear
Leaning with parted lips, some words she spake
In solemn tenour and deep organ tone:
Some mourning words, which in our feeble tongue
Would come in these like accents; O how frail   50
To that large utterance of the early Gods!
'Saturn, look up!—though wherefore, poor old King?
I have no comfort for thee, no not one:
I cannot say, "O wherefore sleepest thou?"
For heaven is parted from thee, and the earth
Knows thee not, thus afflicted, for a God;
And ocean too, with all its solemn noise,
Has from thy sceptre pass'd; and all the air

27 *Amazon*—The Amazons were a race of women-warriors of Asia Minor.
29 *Achilles*—the great Greek warrior who led the Greeks in the Trojan War.
30 *Ixion*—For his insolence to Jove, Ixion was tied to an ever-revolving wheel in Hell.

Is emptied of thy hoary majesty.
Thy thunder, conscious of the new command,   60
Rumbles reluctant o'er our fallen house!
And thy sharp lightning in unpractised hands
Scorches and burns our once serene domain.
O aching time! O moments big as years!
All as ye pass swell out the monstrous truth,
And press it so upon our weary griefs
That unbelief has not a space to breathe.
Saturn, sleep on:—O thoughtless, why did I
Thus violate thy slumbrous solitude?
Why should I ope thy melancholy eyes?   70
Saturn, sleep on! while at thy feet I weep.'

As when, upon a tranced summer-night,
Those green-rob'd senators of mighty woods,
Tall oaks, branch-charmed by the earnest stars,
Dream, and so dream all night without a stir,
Save from one gradual solitary gust
Which comes upon the silence, and dies off,
As if the ebbing air had but one wave;
So came these words and went; the while in tears
She touch'd her fair large forehead to the ground,   80
Just where her falling hair might be outspread
A soft and silken mat for Saturn's feet.
One moon, with alteration slow, had shed
Her silver seasons four upon the night,
And still these two were postured motionless,
Like natural sculpture in cathedral cavern;
The frozen God still couchant on the earth,
And the sad Goddess weeping at his feet:
Until at length old Saturn lifted up
His faded eyes, and saw his kingdom gone,   90
And all the gloom and sorrow of the place,
And that fair kneeling Goddess; and then spake,
As with a palsied tongue, and while his beard

Shook horrid with such aspen-malady:
'O tender spouse of gold Hyperion,
Thea, I feel thee ere I see thy face;
Look up, and let me see our doom in it;
Look up, and tell me if this feeble shape
Is Saturn's; tell me, if thou hear'st the voice
Of Saturn; tell me, if this wrinkling brow,   100
Naked and bare of its great diadem,
Peers like the front of Saturn. Who had power
To make me desolate? whence came the strength?
How was it nurtur'd to such bursting forth,
While Fate seem'd strangled in my nervous grasp?
But it is so; and I am smother'd up,
And buried from all godlike exercise
Of influence benign on planets pale,
Of admonitions to the winds and seas,
Of peaceful sway above man's harvesting,   110
And all those acts which Deity supreme
Doth ease its heart of love in.—I am gone
Away from my own bosom: I have left
My strong identity, my real self,
Somewhere between the throne, and where I sit
Here on this spot of earth. Search, Thea, search!
Open thy eyes eterne, and sphere them round
Upon all space: space starr'd, and lorn of light;
Space region'd with life-air; and barren void;
Spaces of fire, and all the yawn of hell.—   120
Search, Thea, search! and tell me, if thou seest
A certain shape or shadow, making way
With wings or chariot fierce to repossess
A heaven he lost erewhile: it must—it must
Be of ripe progress—Saturn must be King.
Yes, there must be a golden victory;
There must be Gods thrown down, and trumpets blown
Of triumph calm, and hymns of festival
Upon the gold clouds metropolitan,

Voices of soft proclaim, and silver stir   130
Of strings in hollow shells; and there shall be
Beautiful things made new, for the surprise
Of the sky-children; I will give command:
Thea! Thea! Thea! where is Saturn?'

This passion lifted him upon his feet,
And made his hands to struggle in the air,
His Druid locks to shake and ooze with sweat,
His eyes to fever out, his voice to cease.
He stood, and heard not Thea's sobbing deep;
A little time, and then again he snatch'd   140
Utterance thus.—'But cannot I create?
Cannot I form? Cannot I fashion forth
Another world, another universe,
To overbear and crumble this to naught?
Where is another chaos? Where?'—That word
Found way unto Olympus, and made quake
The rebel three.—Thea was startled up,
And in her bearing was a sort of hope,
As thus she quick-voic'd spake, yet full of awe.

'This cheers our fallen house: come to our friends,   150
O Saturn! come away, and give them heart;
I know the covert, for thence came I hither.'
Thus brief; then with beseeching eyes she went
With backward footing through the shade a space:
He follow'd, and she turn'd to lead the way
Through aged boughs, that yielded like the mist
Which eagles cleave upmounting from their nest.

JOHN KEATS

---

145 *chaos*—the confusion of elements from which the world was created.
147 *rebel three*—Jove, Neptune and Pluto, the three divinities who had gained power,
representing the upper world, the seas and the lower world.

John Keats (1795–1821) died just as he had attained his full maturity as a poet after five years of extraordinary and rapid development. His five great odes (*To a Nightingale*, *On a Grecian Urn*, *To Psyche*, *To Autumn* and *On Melancholy*) established his greatness as a poet and emphasised the severity of the loss to English poetry.

Hyperion was an attempt at epic poetry. Keats left it unfinished because, he said, it was too 'Miltonic', and it was published contrary to his wishes. There is no doubt that in style and in the general treatment of the theme, Keats was at the time greatly under the influence of Milton, and, in particular, of *Paradise Lost*. The poem is thus derivative, and in the hands of a lesser poet might well have been merely 'literary'. Keats was too great a poet to take his style from another, for style is, after all, a way of thinking, of feeling and of expression. The style, it has been said, is the man, and Keats did not want to be Milton. He had to create his own style just as Milton had created his. Nevertheless, *Hyperion* remains a noble fragment. The magnificently appropriate imagery, the atmosphere of profound desolation and loss and the statuesque beauty of this scene are not a pale reflection of Milton, but a genuine re-living *through* Milton.

Saturn and the Titans were the primeval gods, the offspring of earth and sky (Tellus and Coelus) who arose from Chaos, the original confusion of the elements. Saturn has been defeated by his son Jupiter, who has turned his own weapon of the thunderbolt against him, and a new order of gods gains power.

ACKNOWLEDGMENTS

FOR permission to include in this anthology various copyright poems the compiler and publishers thank the following:

Messrs. Macmillan & Co. Ltd. for 'Etiquette' from *The Bab Ballads* by Sir W. S. Gilbert (by permission of the author's representatives), for 'The Night of Trafalgar' from *The Dynasts* by Thomas Hardy (by permission of the Trustees of the Hardy estate), and for 'Flannan Isle' by Wilfrid Gibson (by permission of the author); the Society of Authors and Dr. John Masefield, O.M., for his two poems 'The Yarn of the Loch Achray' and 'The Blowing of the Horn'; Messrs. Gerald Duckworth & Co. Ltd. for the poem by Hilaire Belloc entitled 'Lord Lundy' from *Cautionary Verses*; Mr. Edmund Blunden for his poem 'Incident in Hyde Park, 1803'; Messrs. Faber & Faber Ltd. for 'Journey of the Magi' by T. S. Eliot from *Collected Poems 1909–1935*, and for 'O What is That Sound which so Thrills the Ear?' by W. H. Auden from *Collected Shorter Poems 1930–1944*; Mr. Ezra Pound for his poem 'Ballad of the Goodly Fere'; Messrs. Jonathan Cape Ltd. for 'The Nabara' from *Overtures to Death* by C. Day Lewis; and Mr. Robert Graves for 'Welsh Incident' from *Collected Poems of Robert Graves 1914–1947*, published by Messrs. Cassell & Co. Ltd.

INDEX OF FIRST LINES